Sunset

AZALEAS,
RHODODENDRONS
AND CAMELLIAS

BY JOHN R. DUNMIRE, JIM McCAUSLAND,
AND THE EDITORS OF SUNSET BOOKS

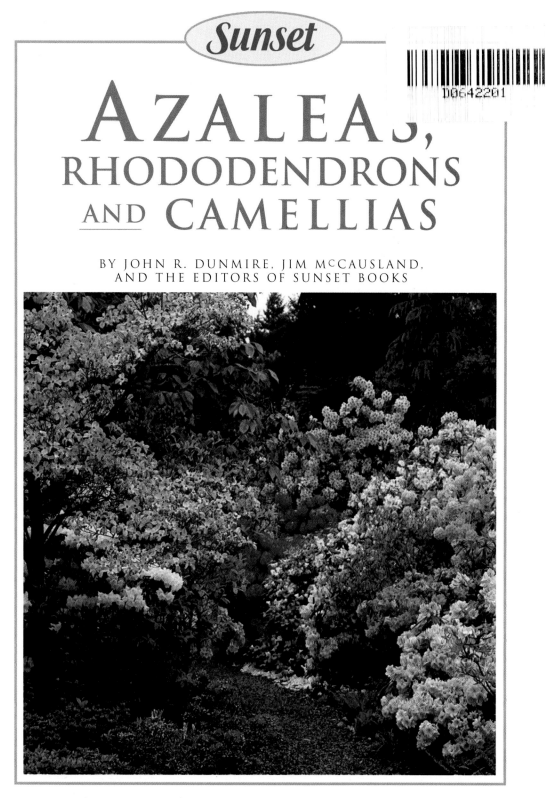

SUNSET BOOKS • MENLO PARK, CALIFORNIA

SPRING CLASSICS

In many ways it makes perfect sense to think of rhododendrons, azaleas, and camellias together. Not only are they botanically related, but most thrive as understory shrubs growing in filtered sun. Their growing ranges also overlap quite a bit—no surprise, since so many of their wild ancestors grow shoulder to shoulder in China, India, and Japan.

For each of these groups—azaleas, rhododendrons, and camellias—spring is the main event. It's then that you'll see some of the most heavily flowering evergreens on the planet, and then that you'll see deciduous azaleas fill our woodlands with their spring fire.

Creating this book took a team effort. We were grateful to be able to call on the expertise of many individuals to ensure that the information we provide is accurate and up to date. We especially want to thank the American Camellia Society, Gerry Bleyer, Joe Blue, Mark Crawford, Jack deAngelis, Michael A. Dirr, Annabelle Fetterman, Peter Girard, Marilee Gray, Harold E. Greer, Steve Hootman, Betty Hotchkiss, Rita Hummell, Len Miller, Dick Muntean, Tom Nuccio, Kristi O'Donnell, Dr. Clifford R. Parks, Jay Pscheidt, Ann Richardson, Ellie Sather, E. White Smith, Hulyn Smith, Lucie Sorenson, Howard Stenn, Tim Thibault, Jerry Turny, and Ted Van Veen.

SUNSET BOOKS

Vice President, Sales: Richard A. Smeby
Editorial Director: Bob Doyle
Production Director: Lory Day
Art Director: Vasken Guiragossian

Staff for this book:

Managing Editor: Marianne Lipanovich
Sunset Books Senior Editor, Gardening: Suzanne Normand Eyre
Contributing Editor: Philip Edinger
Copy Editor and Indexer: Julie Harris
Photo Researcher: Tishana Peebles
Production Coordinator: Patricia S. Williams
Special Contributers: Lisa Anderson, Jean Warboy
Proofreader: Margaret E. Hines

Art Director: Alice Rogers
Page Layouts: Elisa Tanaka
Illustrator: Erin O'Toole
Additional Illustrations: Mimi Osborne, Catherine M. Watters
Computer Production: Fog Press
Cover: *Rhododendron* 'Jingle Bells'. Photograph by Lynne Harrison. Border photograph by David McDonald/PhotoGarden, Inc.

For additional copies of *Azaleas, Rhododendrons, and Camellias,* or any other *Sunset* book, call Leisure Arts, our distribution partners, at 1-800-526-5111.

PHOTOGRAPHERS

Scott Atkinson: 80 left; **R. S. Byther:** 102 top left, 106 left, 107 bottom, 108 bottom; **Ed Carey:** 98 top; **Glenn Christiansen:** 87; **R. Todd Davis:** 34, 49 bottom left, 61 top; **Derek Fell:** 23 top left, 39 middle left, 50 bottom right, 51, 53 top left, 56 all, 93 bottom right, 98 bottom, 99 bottom left; **Harold E. Greer:** 6 left, 7 top, 11, 12 top, 14 top right, 15 top left, top middle, bottom left, bottom middle, 16 top left, top middle, top right, bottom middle, bottom right, 17 top left, top right, 18 top left, top middle, top right, 19 top left, middle left, bottom right, 21 top left, top right, bottom left, 22, 23 top right, bottom right, 27 top , 28 top left, top right, 29, 30 middle, bottom, 36 top, middle, 37 both, 38 top right, bottom left, bottom right, 39 top right, middle right, bottom right, 40 top left, top middle, top right, bottom middle, 41 top left, bottom left, bottom right, 42 top left, top right, bottom right, 43 top middle, bottom middle, 44 top, fourth from top, 45 top, second from top, bottom, 46 top right, 47 all, 48 bottom left, bottom right, 49 top right, bottom right, 50 top left, bottom left, 52 top, middle, 53 bottom left, bottom right, 64 middle, 94, 102 right, 103 top, 109, 110 both, 111 bottom; **Lynne Harrison:** 1, 8 top, 12 bottom, 32 bottom, 46 bottom right, 48 middle left, 52 bottom, 60, 64 top, 65 middle, 67 top, 69 bottom, 74 top left, bottom left, 79, 93 left, 100 bottom; **Saxon Holt:** 2, 3 top, 4–5, 10 top right, 23 bottom left, 57, 66 both, 92, 97, 99 bottom right; **Verna Van de Water Lewis:** 3 bottom, 70–71, 103 bottom left; **Janet Loughrey:** 10 bottom left; 26, 59 bottom; **Ells Marugg:** 15 right; 17 bottom left, bottom right, 23 middle right, 36 bottom, 38 top left, 39 top left, 40 bottom right, 42 bottom left, 43 top left, top right, 44 second from top, 45 third from top, fourth from top, 46 bottom left, 48 top left, 61 bottom, 62 top right, bottom left, bottom right, 63 all, 64 bottom, 65 top, bottom, 69 top, 105; **Stephanie Massey/Susan A. Roth & Co.:** 18 bottom middle; **Jim McCausland:** 73, 76, **David McDonald/PhotoGarden, Inc.:** 50 top right; **Jack McDowell:** 14 top left; **Jerry Pavia:** 10 top left; 14 bottom right, 16 bottom left, 18 bottom right, 27 bottom, 41 top right, 78 bottom, 100 top; **Pamela K. Peirce:** 111 top; **Norman A. Plate:** 44 bottom, 46 top left, 80 right, 88; **Susan A. Roth:** 8 bottom, 14 bottom left, 19 middle right, 21 bottom right, 28 bottom left, 44 third from top; **Michael S. Thompson:** 3 top middle, bottom middle, 6 right, 7 bottom, 19 top right, 20, 24–25, 30 top, 32 top, 33, 35 both, 43 bottom left, 49 top left, 50 top middle, bottom middle, 53 top right, 54–55, 59 top, 62 top left, 67 middle, bottom, 69 middle, 72, 74 top right, 78 top, 83, 85, 86, 91, 93 top right, 99 top left, 103 middle, bottom right, 106 right, 107 top, 108 top.

CONTENTS

The word "azalea" conjures an image of masses of colorful blooms. And that's exactly what azaleas deliver—whether under southern live oaks draped with Spanish moss, in a Pacific Northwest

INTRODUCING
AZALEAS

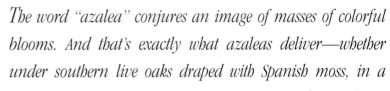

or an East Coast woodland garden, or spilling out of a redwood container on a Southern California patio. Azalea colors range from delicate to garish, hot to cool, solid to variegated. Whatever effect you want, you can be sure that a healthy azalea will be smothered in blossoms in its season.

Azaleas are usually grouped with rhododendrons, and indeed are considered a type of rhododendron. Like rhododendrons, azaleas are forest understory plants, preferring good light but protection from strong, direct sun and from forceful drying winds. Unlike rhododendrons, they tolerate heat, which allows them to thrive in both humid and fairly dry areas of the deep South and central and Southern California.

From their first mention in recorded history through two centuries of avid collecting and hybridizing, azaleas have fascinated growers. That fascination continues today, with even more strains being introduced into our gardens.

Colorful deciduous azalea blooms bring a garden to life in the spring; the foliage provides
a background for other plants throughout summer and fall

What is an Azalea?

A close comparison of azaleas' and rhododendrons' flowers and foliage shows why the two plants are in the same botanical family. In fact, it was once thought that one of the only consistent differences was that azaleas have 5 stamens, whereas rhododendrons have 10 or more. Actually, the differences between the two are not even that constant. Nevertheless, their general appearance makes them easily distinguishable, with few exceptions.

Deciduous azaleas add a wide range
of colors to the azalea color palette.

Pontic azalea
(Rhododendron luteum)

From the gardener's viewpoint, azaleas differ enough from most popular rhododendrons to be treated as distinct plants that just happen to prefer much the same culture (see pages 70–111). The rhododendron is commonly thought of as a massive, large-leafed shrub with heavy trusses of flowers at the branch ends. Azaleas are considered less substantial plants with smaller, thinner leaves and sheets of bloom. The categories aren't rigid, however, and some azaleas look a lot like rhododendrons.

There are two main types of azaleas: evergreen and deciduous. The evergreen types—the azaleas most commonly sold in florists' shops—are hybrids of species from China, Japan, Korea, and Taiwan. Colors include pinks and reds, orange red, lavender, purple, and white—but not yellow. The deciduous species, more widespread in nature, are found in China and Japan, as well as southern Europe; one species is native to the west coast of North America, and more than half hail from the eastern United States and Canada. Colors include soft and bright tones of yellow, orange, and red in addition to shades of pink, white, and lavender. Some deciduous species and hybrids are notably fragrant. Before the annual autumn leaf drop, many produce a second burst of color from foliage that turns yellow, rusty orange, or autumnal red.

Discovery and Development

The recorded history of azaleas begins around 400 B.C. with an account of Greek soldiers who became dangerously ill after eating honey made from nectar of the Pontic azalea *(Rhododendron luteum),* which was growing where the troops had camped along the Black Sea. Three hundred years later, a Roman army was massacred at almost the same location, the troops having become stupefied after eating honey from the same source. Azaleas' potency even has a place in Greek mythology: as reported in Robert Graves' *Hercules, My Shipmate,* Jason and the Argonauts suffered the same ailment—a sort of paralysis coupled with disorientation and mania—when their companion Butes the beekeeper found similar honey and distributed it to the crew.

The entry of azaleas into Western horticultural history began during the 18th and 19th centuries with the English, who collected species from their various colonies while they were building their empire. By the late 1700s many native American azaleas (all deciduous) had reached English gardens—enthusiastically sent to the mother country by plant collectors who explored the territory from New England through the Appalachian Mountains to the southern Gulf Coast. Notable among these collectors was pioneer American botanist and traveler John Bartram, who sent three azaleas, including the spectacular flame azalea *(R. calendulaceum)*, an Appalachian species with scarlet, orange, or yellow flowers. By that time, the infamous Pontic azalea was also growing in England.

In the early years the English grew these deciduous azaleas in greenhouses, chiefly because the plants lacked the formality that was fashionable in the gardens of that time. As landscape design subsequently grew more "natural," deciduous azaleas found a place in shrubbery borders and woodland gardens. The plants were far happier here, where rain, wind, and seasonal variations in temperature were to their liking.

The East India companies of Great Britain and Holland also imported a number of Asiatic azaleas (both deciduous and evergreen sorts) to Europe during the 18th and 19th centuries; among them were some Japanese azaleas obtained via China or Indonesia (the East Indies), since Japan was at that time virtually closed to trade with the Western world. Dutch merchantmen sailing from Batavia (now Djakarta) in Indonesia brought back plants that were christened *Azalea indica*, a name still often used (erroneously) to describe certain of the larger evergreen azaleas. These, too, were greenhouse subjects.

By the 1820s many species of both deciduous and evergreen azaleas were available to European horticulturists, who eagerly took up the challenge of raising hybrid offspring from deliberate crosses.

TOP: Flame azalea *(Rhododendron calendulaceum)*
BOTTOM: Western azalea (*Rhododendron occidentale* 'Centennial')

NINETEENTH-CENTURY GROUNDWORK

In the first years of azalea hybridizing, Belgium led other countries in the production of new varieties, many of which survive today in the evergreen Belgian Indica hybrids and the deciduous Ghent hybrids. Throughout the 19th century, additional species were sent from Asia to Belgium, Britain, Holland, and France, and were immediately recruited into hybridizing programs.

As more and more azaleas were collected from the wild, botanists and horticulturists realized that a number of Asiatic "species" were actually natural hybrids, some were just varying forms of a single widespread species, and still others were old garden hybrids developed in Japan during its centuries of isolation. Conversely, some American plants sent to England that were thought to represent a single species turned out, after careful study, to represent a number of different, though similar, species. (The ancestries of both evergreen and deciduous hybrids are complex, and the uncertain parentage of some plants makes it difficult to sort out exact backgrounds for today's hybrids.)

In the mid-1800s, the introduction to England of America's western azalea *(R. occidentale)* added yet another dimension to deciduous azalea breeding. To the typical yellow, orange, and red hybrids of the Chinese and Japanese deciduous azaleas (and, in some cases, the flame azalea *R. calendulaceum*), *R. occidentale* added soft pink, salmon, cream, and white. It left its imprint on blossom form, too, producing broader petals and blooms with a substantial squared-off appearance— a look readily apparent in today's Knap Hill, Exbury, and similar strains—that was notably different from the earlier, narrow-petaled hybrids.

AZALEA FAMILY TREE

Properly, all azaleas are rhododendrons. But the extensive plant collecting done in Asia during the late 19th and early 20th centuries revealed the great number of species in the genus *Rhododendron* (upward of 900), as well as the variation in appearance among these plants: from heathlike ground covers to tropical-looking trees. Despite the botanical affinities between azaleas and all the other rhododendrons, amateurs and botanists alike realized the need to classify the species in a way that would acknowledge the underlying relationship but categorize the various differences among them.

Until recently, the most widely used system was the one devised by Sir Isaac Bayley Balfour. He divided the genus *Rhododendron* into a number of series, each containing from one to several species that appeared to be closely related. With few exceptions, each series was named for one of its prominent species; if a series contained many species, it was further divided into smaller, more closely knit subseries.

The Azalea series is one that doesn't bear the name of a prominent species. In this group are all the special rhododendrons that the gardening public knows as azaleas. Botanists now place the azaleas into two subgenera: *Pentanthera* includes the deciduous azaleas that we grow in our gardens, while *Tsutsusi* includes all the evergreen azaleas plus a few deciduous species rarely seen outside special collections.

Today, the original series system is being revamped according to contemporary research that is realigning some of the species' affinities. But the basic series concept still provides an organizational framework that will accommodate future adjustments and additions.

Ever-increasing azalea varieties are resulting in their expanded use in garden design.

TWENTIETH-CENTURY REFINEMENTS

By 1900 all the basic parent species of present deciduous azalea hybrids had been assembled and crossed with one another. Most improved hybrids produced since then are still derived from the same species. One notable exception includes the work recently done (and still continuing) with hybridizing superior selections of North American azalea species. Some resulting hybrids have been notably cold-hardy (the Northern Lights series) and some unusually fragrant (the Viscosum hybrids), while others have proved resistant to the summer heat and humidity of the South.

Although most evergreen azaleas are the result of breeding hybrids with other hybrids, either within a strain or between strains, this century has seen the infusion of new blood from *R. yedoense poukhanense* (which conferred cold-hardiness) and other azalea species. For a more complete description of the various groups of azalea hybrids, see pages 12 and 21.

Azaleas, hostas, and hellebores brighten a shady garden path.

AZALEA COUNTRY

Native azalea species grow in many parts of the United States and in Canada. The West Coast grows both evergreen and deciduous azaleas. Central and Southern California coastal areas can grow even the tender Belgian Indica and Southern Indica kinds, as well as the hardier evergreens. The latter also thrive in the Pacific Northwest. Deciduous azaleas grow in the Columbia River Basin (the hardiest evergreen kinds need careful siting and shelter there). Denver and its vicinity can support deciduous azaleas of the Northern Lights series.

The Gulf Coast is home to many deciduous azalea species. The evergreen Southern Indicas also thrive there, as well as many of the hardier evergreens, whose reach extends northward along the Atlantic Coast and the Piedmont to the Chesapeake Bay region, eastern Pennsylvania, New Jersey, the New York City area, and along the New England coast as far as Maine (where they require protection from winter wind and sun). The hardier evergreens also grow along the shores of Lake Erie and southwestward to St. Louis. Deciduous azaleas of the Northern Lights series now thrive and bloom in much of Minnesota.

"Azalea Country," therefore, is determined by which azaleas you want to grow and how much special attention (in less favorable areas) you're willing to give them. For growing in the ground, evergreen sorts are largely restricted to regions where winters are not severe and where proximity to large bodies of water moderate temperatures and provide atmospheric humidity. Deciduous sorts extend the boundaries into chilly-winter northern states, the midwestern heartland, the Great Lakes and St. Lawrence–influenced southern Ontario and Quebec, and the Maritime Provinces. In other areas, dry atmosphere and alkaline soil, combined with either extreme winter cold or intense summer heat, rule out success—or even survival—for azaleas. It is wise to consult your most knowledgeable local nursery before you buy.

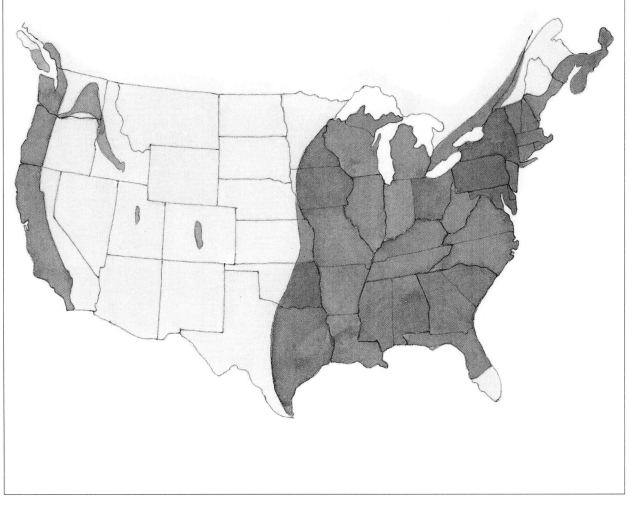

AZALEAS IN THE LANDSCAPE

If you've ever been to a florist shop, likely as not you've seen azaleas. But if that's the extent of your exposure to azaleas, you're in for a surprise when you see them in the landscape.

'Ward's Ruby' azalea and silky wisteria edge a terrace balustrade.

TOP: Azaleas and 'White Emperor' tulips add a splash of color.

BOTTOM: A mixed azalea and rhododendron border provides seasonal bloom.

Though azaleas can't offer quite the range of plant, foliage, and flower types that rhododendrons do, they can easily fit into as many landscape situations. In addition to the deciduous azaleas, which provide a second season of interest with colorful autumn foliage, there are low-growing evergreen varieties that can serve as ground covers; compact azaleas, and ones that are tall and willowy; plants wider than they are tall or the reverse; and some that will attain the size of small trees when mature. With such a variety of raw material, you can plant borders, hedges, barriers, or backdrops of diverse proportions—all of which will blaze with color in season and have a neat appearance during the rest of the year.

CHOICE LOCATIONS

Azaleas can enhance any garden. They especially look at home in plantings near water: beside ponds, their reflections double the effect (and the plants thrive in the humidity).

They're also prime subjects for Asian-style gardens because their branch structure can be guided easily into characteristic horizontal planes or sheared into mounds to resemble rocks or hills. In many classic Japanese gardens, azalea flowers are a bonus—the closely sheared foliage mound being of principal interest of the gardener.

Singly or in groups, azaleas in containers (see page 97) will dramatically enhance a patio, terrace, deck, or porch. And like their rhododendron relatives, azaleas are unexcelled as components of lightly shaded woodland gardens.

Massed plantings are especially beautiful, and notable examples of azalea valleys and azalea hillsides may be seen in large public gardens. In such landscapes, color blending and contrast are important. For best effect, don't place massed plantings of a single color near a similar group with a conflicting color. Rather, use masses or drifts of white-flowered varieties to enhance pinks, purples, and reds, and to separate warring hues.

Many low-growing or trailing evergreen azaleas are useful in rock gardens or as small-scale ground covers. These may also be planted to trail over walls or ledges, or planted in hanging baskets (as can many of the larger evergreen azaleas, given some pinching and training). Evergreen azaleas can also be grown as standards (small single-stemmed trees) or trained on trellises.

AZALEA SHOWCASE

These 13 pages contain descriptions of almost 200 evergreen and deciduous azaleas. Although nothing like a comprehensive catalog—Fred C. Galle's monumental Azaleas *lists thousands, especially evergreen sorts—these listings do cover the varieties most likely to be found in nurseries. Many other varieties may be available in some areas, and mail order sources will provide even more.*

Rhododendron mucronatum

EVERGREEN AZALEAS

The evergreen azaleas fall into more than a dozen groups and species, although an increasing number of hybrids have such mixed parentage that they don't conveniently fit into any group. Except as noted, bloom season is early, from March through April. In greenhouses, plants can be forced for winter bloom.

EVERGREEN AZALEA SPECIES

The vast majority of evergreen azaleas are hybrids. The few true species maintained in cultivation are grown in botanical collections or used as breeding stock. Many other so-called species are either cutting-grown plants from selected clones of a species, or else plants originally introduced as species but later found to be old Japanese garden plants of unknown parentage. The following listings include species of all three types.

R. indicum. Not to be confused with Southern Indica hybrids. This species exists in gardens only in one or two of its varieties. One is 'Balsaminaeflorum', also known as 'Rosaeflora', a low-growing, compact plant that produces fully double 1½-inch red flowers late in the season, from May through July. 'Flame Creeper', low and spreading with single orange red flowers, is a useful rock garden plant. Hardy to −5°F/−21°C.

R. kaempferi. TORCH AZALEA. Probably the hardiest evergreen or semi-evergreen azalea (to −15°F/−26°C). Deciduous at the limit of its hardiness. Native over a wide area in Japan. It grows to a twiggy 8 feet in height. Flowers are 1½ to 2 inches long and red to pink.

R. kiusianum. Japanese species with many named varieties. All are compact and dense-growing, bloom young and heavily, and are choice subjects for bonsai, rock garden, or foreground planting. Leaves are small and may drop in cold weather. Inch-wide flowers in early spring may be purple, red, pink, or white. The selection 'Komo Kulshan', with pale pink flowers tipped deep rose, is considered choice. Hardy to −10°F/−23°C.

R. linearifolium. SPIDER AZALEA. Properly called *R. macrosepalum* 'Lineari-folium'. This novelty is a 3- to 6-foot spreading shrub with hairy 2-inch leaves and freak-ish purplish pink to purplish red flowers cut into narrow, 1½-inch segments that look like straps. Hardy to about 10°F/−12°C.

R. mucronatum. SNOW AZALEA. Not a species but an old Japanese garden plant. It has also been called *R. indica alba* and *R. ledifolia alba,* but its proper name should be 'Mucronatum'. It grows 6 to 10 feet tall and as wide, with hairy 1½- to 2-inch leaves and large (to 3 inches) white flowers in spring. Flowers of the variety 'Sekidera' are flushed or

TOP: 'Flame Creeper'
BOTTOM: *Rhododendron yedoense poukhanense*

blotched with purplish pink. 'Delaware Valley White' is said to be hardier. 'Indica Rosea' is flushed with pink. Hardy to 5°F/−15°C.

R. yedoense poukhanense. KOREAN AZALEA. A 5- to 6-foot shrub from Korea with 2-inch flowers of rose to lilac. It is evergreen, but loses leaves in the coldest winter climates. Hardy to −15°F/−26°C.

EVERGREEN AZALEA HYBRIDS

Hybridizers have worked with evergreen azaleas for more than 150 years. The usual objective for each hybridizer was to produce a group of plants that would perform well in a particular situation: in the greenhouse, in cold-winter climates, or in hot-summer territory. As a result, many evergreen azalea hybrids sold today can be separated into reasonably distinct groups whose varieties have similar climatic tolerances and often similar growth and flower types.

Listed here are descriptions of the principal evergreen types, each with the code abbreviation used in the variety listings that follow. If you know the class to which a new variety belongs, you may be reasonably sure of its performance.

BI—Belgian Indica. Developed primarily for greenhouse growing, but in mild regions where the lowest temperatures don't fall below 20°F/−7°C they may also serve as landscape plants. Their evergreen foliage is lush and full, and plants show a profusion of semidouble or double (rarely single) flowers during the blooming season. They are often available in pots from florists, nurseries, and even supermarkets. As house plants they are difficult to maintain unless given cool, bright conditions and careful watering and feeding.

Be—Beltsville. Resemble Glenn Dale hybrids and are hardy to 0°F/−18°C. They derive their hardiness from *R. kaempferi*.

Br, GC, and N—Brooks, Gold Cup, and Nuccio. Three hybrid groups developed in California and hardy to about 20°F/−7°C. The Brooks hybrids, from the state's central valley, were developed to tolerate the hot, dry summer climate there. The Gold Cup hybrids combine the large flowers of Belgian Indicas with the vigor of the Rutherfordianas. The Nuccio hybrids are of a mixed ancestry that includes Belgian Indicas and Kurumes; they're especially well adapted to the mild and dry climate of Southern California.

G—Gable. Developed in southeastern Pennsylvania as evergreen azaleas of the Kurume type that would take 0°F/−18°C temperatures. Since *R. kaempferi* is an ancestor of all, the Gable hybrids are really a special group of Kaempferi hybrids. In temperatures at the low range of their tolerance, these plants may lose some foliage. Bloom is heavy from April through May.

Gi—Girard. Ohio-bred hybrids representing selections from the Gable group crossed with other hybrids. Most are hardy to −5°F/−21°C or somewhat colder.

Gl—Glenn Dale. Developed to get the color and flower size of the southern azaleas on plants that would be hardy (to 0°F/−18°C) in the mid-Atlantic states. They take their name from the site of the U.S. Division of Plant Exploration and Introduction station in Maryland. Some plants grow tall and rangy, others low and compact; some have small leaves like the Kurumes, others large leaves. Growth rates vary widely from rapid to slow. These hybrids grow well in half sun, and some varieties will take full sun. During cold winters some leaves will drop. Back Acres hybrids, developed from the Glenn Dales, were created at Pass Christian, Mississippi, to perform well in that part of the South.

Ka—Kaempferi. Developed in part from *R. kaempferi* and similar to the Kurumes but taller and of more open growth. Plants are hardy to −15°F/−26°C but nearly deciduous in the coldest winters. Flowers are profuse in early spring. Varieties sold as Vuykiana hybrids also come under the Kaempferi heading, and all Gable hybrids are *R. kaempferi* derivatives.

K—Kurume. Garden favorites in Japan for more than a century, and developed there for outdoor culture. They grow rather compactly and are densely covered with small leaves. Although the flowers are small, they come out in masses, often in attractive tiers that suggest the plants in Japanese prints. Kurume azaleas will take temperatures down to 5°F/−15°C and grow well outdoors in half sun, but they cannot endure hot, dry summer winds. In humid, cool climates some varieties thrive in full sun. In cold-winter climates they should be protected against bright sun and wind by burlap screens. They are excellent container plants and favored bonsai subjects, and are particularly effective massed on banks.

M—Macrantha. Includes plants that are sometimes referred to as Gumpo, Chugai, and Satsuki hybrids. They are hardy to around 5°F/–15°C and include low-growing and dwarf varieties. All these hybrids are late bloomers, flowering well into June, with flowers larger than those of the Kurumes.

Mo—Monrovia. Developed by Monrovia Nursery in Southern California by using Belgian Indica and Southern Indica azaleas as parents. They resemble Southern Indicas and thrive in the warm, dry California climate. Hardy to 10°F/–12°C.

NT—North Tisbury. Dwarf azaleas developed on Martha's Vineyard, Massachusetts, with the prostrate *R. naka-barai* in their ancestry. They are useful in the rock garden and also are good choices small-scale ground covers. Hardy to –9°F/–23°C.

P—Pericat. A series of azaleas developed in Pennsylvania for greenhouse forcing. Possibly hybrids of Belgian Indica and Kurume varieties, they look much like the Kurumes and are about as hardy.

RH—Robin Hill. Resemble the Macranthas in blooming late and producing large flowers, but hardier to cold (to 0°F/–18°C, probably colder) and more resistant to heat. Most are 2 to 4 feet tall; some are dwarf.

R—Rutherfordiana. American equivalents of the Belgian Indicas, developed for greenhouse forcing. Like the Belgian Indicas, they are good landscape subjects where temperatures don't go below 20°F/–7°C. Plants are bushy, 2 to 4 feet tall, with handsome foliage. Flower size is intermediate, between the Belgian Indicas and Kurumes; blossoms may be single, semidouble, or double.

Sh—Shammarello. Ohio-bred plants resembling the Gable hybrids but hardier (to –5°F/–21°C or somewhat colder). The very hardy Korean azalea *(R. yedoense poukhanense)* is one parent of many varieties.

SI—Southern Indica. The garden azaleas famous throughout the Deep South. Originally they were selected from the Belgian Indica varieties that were more rugged and better able to perform in full sun than most other azaleas. Somewhat hardier than Belgian Indicas, they will take temperatures from 20° to 10°F/–7° to –12°C, although some will split bark at 20°F/–7°C and most white-flowered varieties will suffer frozen buds at that temperature. In general, the Southern Indicas grow faster, more vigorously, and taller than other evergreen azalea types. You may find them sold in California as "sun azaleas." They are used for massing and as individual specimens, either as shrubs, standards, or espaliers.

AZALEA FLOWER FORMS

A typical azalea flower has five petals joined at the base to form a tube, giving the flower a trumpet or funnel shape. At the base of the trumpet or funnel is an outer ring of very small green sepals that are joined together like a collar. In the center of the flower are five stamens—sometimes more—but in multiples of five. This arrangement constitutes a *single* flower. In many cases the filaments of the stamens become petal-like; then you have a *semidouble* or *double* flower, depending on the number of stamens that have a petal-like form.

The term *hose-in-hose* refers to the outer ring of normally small green sepals that becomes large, petal-like, and showy. Because they're joined into a tube at the base (like the petals), the actual flower appears to be inside another. In this case the stamen filaments may also become petal-like; then you have a flower that is *semidouble hose-in-hose* or *double hose-in-hose*.

Single   Semidouble

Double   Hose-in-hose

Semidouble hose-in-hose   Double hose-in-hose

TOP: 'Alaska'
BOTTOM: 'Appleblossom'

TOP: 'Albert and Elizabeth'
BOTTOM: 'Ben Morrison'

ALASKA. R.
White single, semidouble, or double flowers with chartreuse blotch. October/November–April bloom.

ALBERT AND ELIZABETH. BI.
White double flowers with salmon pink edges. October–May bloom.

ALBION. R.
White hose-in-hose flowers with green throat. March–April bloom.

ALEXANDER. NT.
Reddish orange single flowers; bronze fall foliage. May–June bloom.

APHRODITE. Gl.
Rose pink single flowers on a spreading plant. Blooms in March.

APPLEBLOSSOM. K.
White single flowers tipped pink. March–April bloom.

AVALANCHE. K.
Pure white single flowers. Sheets of bloom in March and April.

BABY JILL. GC.
Light orchid pink double flowers, darker toward edges. February–April bloom.

BALSAMINAEFLORUM. See *R. indicum*, page 11.

BEN MORRISON. Gl.
Large (2½-inch), deep pink, single flowers with pronounced white margin that may not become evident until plant is established. Erect plant to 4 to 6 feet tall or more. March–May bloom.

BETTY ANNE VOSS. RH.
Large, soft pink, hose-in-hose flowers. May–June bloom.

BLAAUW'S PINK. K.
Deep pink hose-in-hose flowers with darker blotch. March–May bloom.

BLUE DANUBE. Ka.
Large, reddish violet, single flowers. March–April bloom.

BLUSHING BRIDE. BI.
Very large, pale pink, semidouble flowers. November/December–May bloom.

BUCCANEER. Gl.
Orange red single flowers. April–May bloom.

BUNKA (BUNKWA). M.
Large, salmon pink, single flowers with deeper pink edges. May–June bloom.

CALIFORNIA SUNSET. BI.
Salmon pink double flowers with paler edges. October–May bloom.

CAROLINE GABLE. G.
Brilliant pink hose-in-hose flowers. March–April bloom.

CASABLANCA. Be.
White single flowers in clusters of 3 to 7. 'Casablanca Improved' has larger flowers. March–April bloom.

CASCADE. Sh.
Medium-size single white flowers. April–May bloom.

CHIMES. BI.
Large, dark red, semidouble flowers. November/December–March bloom.

CONGO. RH.
Large (to 2½ inches), bright reddish purple, single flowers. Plants are compact, reaching 16 inches in height with a 3-foot spread. April–June bloom.

TOP: 'Blue Danube'
BOTTOM: 'Elsie Lee'

TOP: 'Coral Bells'
BOTTOM: 'Fedora'

'Formosa'

CONSTANCE. R.

Large, pinkish lavender, single flowers. November/December–March/April bloom.

CONVERSATION PIECE. RH.

Large, white, single flowers prominently marked with purplish red; some flowers are pure white. May–June bloom.

CORAL BELLS (KIRIN). K.

Small, coral pink, hose-in-hose flowers; small leaves. December–March/April bloom.

DAYSPRING. Gl.

Medium, single purplish pink flowers with white center, greenish yellow blotch. April–May bloom.

DELAWARE VALLEY WHITE. See *R. mucronatum*, page 11.

DELICATISSIMA. K.

Small to medium, single white flowers flushed pink. March–April bloom.

DOROTHY GISH. R.

Brick red hose-in-hose flowers on a compact plant with dark, glossy leaves. December–April bloom.

DOROTHY HAYDEN. RH.

Large, white, single flowers with green throat. This is a small plant, only 1½ feet tall, 2 feet across. May–June bloom.

DUC DE ROHAN. SI.

Salmon pink single flowers with rose throat. December–April/May bloom.

EASTER BONNET. GC.

Purplish pink semidouble flowers with white throat and greenish flecks. November/December–April bloom.

EASTER PARADE. GC.

Large, pink, ruffled hose-in-hose flowers with white mottling. March–April bloom.

ELSIE LEE. Sh.

Large, lavender pink, frilled semi-double flowers. April–May bloom.

EUREKA. Be.

Small, light purplish pink, hose-in-hose flowers. Profuse March–April bloom.

EVEREST. Gl.

White single flowers with chartreuse blotch. May bloom.

FEDORA. Ka.

Large, salmon to deep rose pink, single flowers. March–April bloom.

FIELDER'S WHITE. SI.

White, frilled, single flowers blotched with chartreuse. March–April bloom.

FIRELIGHT. R.

Bright red hose-in-hose flowers. November/December–April bloom.

FLAME CREEPER. See *R. indicum*, page 11.

TOP: 'Geisha'
BOTTOM: 'George Lindley Taber'

TOP: 'Girard's Hotshot'
BOTTOM: 'Gumpo Pink'

TOP: 'Hi Gasa'
BOTTOM: 'Hilda Niblett'

FORMOSA (PHOENICIA). SI.

Large, lavender purple, single flowers on a large plant. Somewhat more cold tolerant than most Southern Indicas. March–April bloom.

GEISHA. Gl.

White single flowers blotched chartreuse and flecked or striped reddish purple. March–April bloom.

GEORGE LINDLEY TABER. SI.

Large (to 3½ inches) single flowers variously described as white flushed lavender pink with a darker blotch, or as purplish pink with a white rim. Large, fast-growing plant. March–May bloom.

GIRARD'S FUCHSIA. Gi.

Deep reddish purple, wavy-edged, single flowers with lighter markings. April–May bloom.

GIRARD'S HOT SHOT. Gi.

Deep orange red, wavy-edged, single flowers. Shiny foliage turns red in fall. April–May bloom.

GIRARD'S ROBERTA. Gi.

Deep pink, ruffled double flowers. April–May bloom.

GLACIER. Gl.

Large, white, single flowers; shiny leaves. March–April bloom.

GLORY OF SUNNINGHILL. SI.

Bright orange red single flowers. April–May bloom.

GUMPO PINK. M.

Medium-size, coral or salmon pink, single flowers with deeper flecks. Mutation of the white variety 'Gumpo'. May–June bloom.

GUY YERKES. Be.

Salmon to deep pink hose-in-hose flowers, fading lighter. March–April bloom.

HELEN CURTIS. Sh.

Large, pure white, frilled semidouble flowers. April–May bloom.

HERBERT. G.

Reddish purple hose-in-hose flowers with darker blotch. April–May bloom.

HERSHEY RED. K.

Small to medium bright red single flowers. April–May bloom.

HEXE. K.

Crimson red hose-in-hose flowers. Low, spreading plant. March–April bloom.

HI GASA. M.

Very large, deep rose pink, single flowers with dark spotted throats. May–June bloom.

HILDA NIBLETT. RH.

Big (4-inch) single flowers striped deep pink, light pink, and white. May–June bloom.

HINO-CRIMSON. K.

❀ Small, bright red, single flowers. Profuse bloom on a compact plant. Leaves turn red in winter. February–April bloom.

HINODEGIRI. K.

❀ Cherry red flowers hide foliage. Tiered growth habit and red winter foliage. February–April bloom.

HOLLAND. Ka.

❀ Large, bright red, single flowers. March–April bloom.

IMPERIAL COUNTESS. Mo (SI).

❀ Deep salmon pink hose-in-hose flowers. March–April bloom. One of a "family" of hybrids including 'Imperial Duchess', with bright pink double flowers, April–May bloom; 'Imperial Princess', with pink single flowers, March–April bloom; and 'Imperial Queen', with pink double flowers, April–May bloom.

INDICA ALBA, INDICA ROSEA. See *R. mucronatum*, page 11.

IVERYANA. SI.

❀ Large, lavender, single flowers with white edge and purple flecks; some flowers entirely red. April–May bloom.

JEAN HAERENS. BI.

❀ Large, deep rose pink, double flowers. February–April bloom.

JOHN CAIRNS. Ka.

❀ Bright red single flowers. Hardy plant. March–April bloom.

JOSEPH HILL. NT.

❀ Red single flowers covering a low (14-inch), wide (to 5 feet) plant that can be deciduous in colder areas. May–June bloom.

KAEMPO. Macrantha-Kurume hybrid.

❀ Deep purplish pink single flowers with darker spots. Low, compact, hardy plant. April–May bloom.

L. J. BOBBINK. R.

❀ Large, orchid lavender, semidouble flowers. March–April bloom.

LEDIFOLIA ALBA. See *R. mucronatum*, page 11.

LITTLE JOHN. SI.

❀ Very dark red single flowers; scant blooms. Six-foot shrub has reddish purple foliage. April bloom.

LOUISE GABLE. G.

❀ Salmon pink semidouble flowers on a low plant. April–May bloom.

MADONNA. Br.

❀ Large, white, double flowers; light green foliage. December–April bloom.

MARIA DERBY. RH.

❀ Bright orange red hose-in hose flowers on a compact plant. May–June bloom.

MARIE'S CHOICE. Sh.

❀ Medium white single flowers. April–May bloom.

MAY BELLE. Sh.

❀ Medium, deep pink to purplish red, semidouble flowers. April–May bloom.

MEMOIRE JOHN HAERENS (JOHN HAERENS SPORT). BI.

❀ Large, white, double flowers edged with cherry red. March–May bloom.

MISSION BELLS. BI.

❀ Bright red, ruffled, semidouble to double flowers. February–April bloom.

MME. ALFRED SANDER. BI.

❀ Large, rich red, double flowers; compact plant. October–May bloom.

NANCY OF ROBIN HILL. RH.

❀ Large, light pink, semidouble to double flowers with occasional red blotch. Low, compact plant. May–June bloom.

TOP: 'Louise Gable'
BOTTOM: 'Madonna'

TOP: 'Joseph Hill'
BOTTOM: 'Mme. Alfred Sander'

'Purple Splendor' and 'Hino-Crimson'

NUCCIO'S DREAM CLOUDS. N (BI).

Large, white, ruffled double flowers with green throat. December–April bloom.

NUCCIO'S MASTERPIECE. N (BI).

Very large, white, ruffled double flowers. Needs some shade. March–April bloom.

NUCCIO'S MELODY LANE. N (BI).

Large, pale pink, single flowers with spotted rose red throat. Long blooming. December–April/May bloom.

NUCCIO'S PINK BUBBLES. N (BI).

Large, light pink, double flowers; dark foliage. December–April bloom.

NUCCIO'S POLKA. N (M).

Large, orange red, wavy-edged single flowers. March–May bloom.

NUCCIO'S SUNBURST. BI.

Orange red semidouble flowers on a compact plant with dark green foliage. February–April bloom.

OLGA NIBLETT. RH.

Large, white, single flowers with a yellow cast on a 4-foot shrub. April–June bloom.

ORCHIDIFLORA. BI.

Large, orchid pink, semidouble flowers. October–April bloom.

PALESTRINA. Ka.

White single flowers with chartreuse blotch. March–May bloom.

PAUL SCHAEME. BI.

Large, salmon pink to light orange, double flowers. October–April bloom.

PERLE DE SWEYNAERDE. BI.

Large, white, double flowers; dark green foliage. October–April bloom.

PINK CASCADE. NT.

Salmon pink single flowers blotched red on a trailing plant. May–June bloom.

PINK PEARL. K.

Large, soft pink, double blossoms. October–April bloom.

PRIDE OF DORKING. SI.

Bright red single flowers. Erect, compact plant. March–April bloom.

PURITY. R.

White single to semidouble flowers. January–March bloom.

PURPLE SPLENDOR. G.

Red violet, frilled, single or hose-in-hose flowers. Plant is low to medium in height, and spreading. March–April bloom.

RED POPPY. BI.

Very large, dark red, single to semi-double flowers. October–May bloom.

RED WING. BI.

Bright red, ruffled, hose-in-hose flowers. Can take full sun. November/December–April bloom.

REFRAIN. Gl.

Large hose-in-hose flowers may be purplish pink with darker markings to pink with white edging and stripes. Overall effect is rich pink. April–May bloom.

ROBIN HILL GILLIE. RH.

Very large (to 5 inches), salmon pink, single flowers on a compact (2½-foot) plant. May–June bloom.

ROSAEFLORA (BALSAMINAEFLORA). See *R. indicum,* page 11.

TOP: 'Red Poppy'
BOTTOM: 'Rosebud'

TOP: 'Refrain'
BOTTOM: 'Rose Greeley'

ROSEBUD. G.

Small, pink double flowers resembling miniature roses. Low, compact plant. March–April bloom.

ROSE GREELEY. G.

White hose-in-hose flowers blotched chartreuse; fragrant. Dense, spreading plant. March–April bloom.

ROSE QUEEN. R.

Deep pink, semidouble, hose-in-hose flowers with white throat. November/December–April bloom.

RUBY GLOW. See 'Ward's Ruby', below.

SEKIDERA. See *R. mucronatum*, page 11.

SHERWOOD ORCHID. K.

Orchid lavender single flowers with darker blotches. March–April bloom.

SHERWOOD PINK. K.

Small, bright pink, single flowers on a low plant. March–April bloom.

SHERWOOD RED. K.

Brilliant orange red, single flowers. Plant drops leaves at the limit of its hardiness. March–April bloom.

SHINNYO-NO-TSUKI. M.

Large, violet red, single flowers with white centers. April–May bloom.

SIR ROBERT. RH.

Large (to 4 inches) single flowers of palest pink to pink and white. Low, dense plant. May–June bloom.

SNOW. K.

White hose-in-hose flowers; profuse blooms. Dead blossoms hang on plant. March–April bloom.

SOUTHERN CHARM. SI.

Light pink single flowers with deeper blotch. March–April bloom.

TOP: 'Sherwood Orchid'
BOTTOM: 'Shinnyo-No-Tsuki'

TOP: 'Sherwood Red'
BOTTOM: 'Stewartstonian'

STEWARTSTONIAN. G.

Bright red single flowers; reddish winter foliage. Exceptionally hardy. March–April bloom.

SUN VALLEY. GC.

Large, creamy white to pale yellow, hose-in-hose flowers. March–May bloom.

TACHISENE. Ka.

The double form of *R. kaempferi* on page 11.

TRADITION (ROEHRS TRADITION). Ka.

Small, medium-pink hose-in-hose flowers. Low, broad plant. May–July bloom.

UNSURPASSABLE. Gi.

Medium to large, deep pink, single frilly flowers. Broad, dense plant. March–May bloom.

VERVAENEANA. BI.

Deep pink double flowers with white edges and rose red throat. February–May bloom.

WARD'S RUBY. Gi.

Small, bright dark red, single flowers covering a low- to medium-spreading, dense-growing plant. Also

known as 'Ruby Glow'. Displays good maroon fall foliage color. February–April bloom.

WHITE APRIL. SI.

Large, white, single flowers; upright plant. February–March bloom.

WHITE GISH. R.

White hose-in-hose flowers on a compact plant with shiny foliage. February–April bloom.

WILLIAM VAN ORANGE. BI.

Large, orange red, ruffled single flowers. February–April bloom.

'Ward's Ruby'

Deciduous Azaleas

Very few deciduous shrubs can equal deciduous azaleas in show and range of color. Even flowers of their evergreen relatives can't match them in the yellow, orange, and flame red range or in bicolor contrasts. Fall foliage is often brilliant orange red to maroon. Deciduous azaleas generally tend to be hardier than most evergreen types.

Deciduous Azalea Species

Most deciduous azaleas on the market are hybrids, but plants of many species are available. Although some American species were introduced into cultivation quite early and extensively used in early hybridizing, interest was greater in Europe than here. A revival of interest in the American species has led to much work in selection and hybridizing. These American azaleas are often known as honeysuckles for their fragrance. Many of these plants are recent introductions in short supply and often available only in the regions where the hybridizing is being done.

Deciduous hybrid azaleas in bloom

R. alabamense. ALABAMA AZALEA. Grows 2 to 6 feet tall and spreads by suckers to form large clumps. Flowers are white with a yellow blotch and fragrant. Native to Alabama, Georgia, and South Carolina. Hardy to −5°F/−21°C.

R. arborescens. SWEET AZALEA. Large (to 15 feet) shrub blooming after leaves appear. Flowers are white, sometimes tinted pink, with a yellow blotch and strong fragrance. Native from New York to Alabama, Kentucky, and Tennessee. Hardy to −10°F/−23°C.

R. atlanticum. COASTAL AZALEA. Low (1- to 2-foot-tall), suckering shrub with white (rarely pink-tinted), fragrant flowers that appear before or with the leaves. Native to lowlands from southern Pennsylvania to Georgia. Hardy to −15°F/−26°C.

R. austrinum. FLORIDA AZALEA. Grows 8 to 10 feet tall. Fragrant flowers appear before leaves in clusters of up to 15 and range from cream to yellow, pink, orange, or red. Native to northern and western Florida and southern parts of Georgia, Alabama, and Mississippi. Hardy to 5°F/−15°C.

R. bakeri. CUMBERLAND AZALEA. Grows 3 to 8 feet tall and produces 1½-inch flowers after leaves appear. Colors range from yellow through orange to red. Native to mountains of Kentucky and Tennessee to northern Georgia and Alabama. Hardy to −15°F/−26°C. Does not tolerate heat.

R. calendulaceum. FLAME AZALEA. Grows 4 to 8 feet tall and produces extremely showy yellow, orange, or red flowers before the leaves appear. A very important parent of many hybrid deciduous azaleas. Hardy to −25°F/−32°C.

R. canadense. RHODORA. Grows 3 to 4 feet tall, less in open situations and poor soils. Flowers appear just as leaves begin to open and are deep purple in color, with narrow, strap-shaped petals; there is a white form. Native from Labrador to northern Pennsylvania and New Jersey. It can grow in deep shade, wet soil, or windswept, rocky, open situations. Needs cool climate. Hardy to −25°F/−32°C.

R. canescens. PIEDMONT AZALEA. Grows to 10, sometimes 15 feet tall and produces clusters of small (to 1½ inches), fragrant, white to pink flowers before or with the leaves. Native from North Carolina, south and west to Oklahoma, Arkansas, and East Texas. Hardy to −5°F/−21°C.

R. flammeum. OCONEE AZALEA. May be low or tall. Flowers open as leaves expand and are yellowish orange to orange or red. They are not fragrant. Native to fairly low elevations in Georgia and South Carolina. They are hardy to −15°F/−26°C and exceptionally heat tolerant.

R. japonicum. JAPANESE AZALEA. Grows 4 to 6 feet tall and blooms before leaves appear. Flowers 2 to 3 inches broad may be yellow, orange, or red, and come in clusters of 6 to 12. Native to Japan. Widely used in hybridizing and effective in mass plantings. Hardy to −10°F/−23°C.

R. luteum. PONTIC AZALEA. Grows to 8 feet or more and produces fragrant, yellow, single flowers with a darker blotch; blooms come before the leaves appear. Native to Asia Minor and Eastern Europe. Hardy to −15°F/−26°C. An ancestor of Ghent hybrids.

R. molle. CHINESE AZALEA. A 4- to 5-foot-tall shrub that produces flowers in trusses of up to 20 before leaves appear. Flowers are yellow with faint green spotting in the throat. Hardy to −10°F/−23°C. An important parent of the Mollis hybrids.

R. mucronulatum. Although generally regarded as an azalea, this plant is a deciduous rhododendron. Grows to 6 feet tall and broad. Blooms very early (with forsythia), with a profuse show of reddish purple flowers nearly 2 inches wide. 'Cornell Pink' has rosy pink flowers. Native to northern China, Korea, and Japan. Hardy to −25°F/−32°C.

R. oblongifolium. TEXAS AZALEA. Grows to 6 feet tall and produces clusters of fragrant 1-inch white flowers after leaves appear. Native to East Texas, Oklahoma, and Arkansas. Hardy to −5°F/−21°C.

R. occidentale. WESTERN AZALEA. Grows 6 to 10 feet tall and blooms after leaves have expanded. Flowers are white to pinkish white with a prominent yellow blotch and fragrant.

Selections have been made that show superior flower size and coloring, often with a mixture of red. 'Leonard Frisbie' and 'Washington Centennial' are superior forms. Hardy to −5°F/−21°C.

R. periclymenoides (R. nudiflorum). PINXTERBLOOM AZALEA. Grows 2 to 3 feet tall, occasionally taller, and spreads by suckering. Fragrant pale to deep pink flowers appear after the leaves. Commonly called honeysuckle in its native home—Massachusetts to Ohio and North Carolina. Hardy to −15°F/−26°C.

R. prinophyllum (R. roseum). ROSESHELL AZALEA. Grows 4 to 8 feet tall and occasionally much taller. The bright pink (occasionally white) flowers appear before or with the leaves and have a strong clove fragrance. Native from eastern Canada to Virginia, Missouri, and Oklahoma. Hardy to −25°F/−32°C. An important parent of the Northern Lights series of hybrid azaleas.

R. schlippenbachii. ROYAL AZALEA. Grows 6 to 8 feet tall and produces large (2- to 4-inch), pure light pink, fragrant flowers in clusters of 3 to 6 as the leaves are expanding. Leaves show brilliant fall color. Native to Korea and Manchuria. Hardy to −20°F/−29°C.

R. viscosum. SWAMP AZALEA. Grows 5 to 8 feet tall or more. Flowers are white, sometimes pinkish, 2 inches long, sticky on the outside, and powerfully clove scented. They appear after the leaves are fully developed in late spring or early summer. Native to damp or wet sites from Maine to Florida and west to Louisiana and Texas. Hardy to −25°F/−32°C.

TOP: *Rhododendron atlanticum*
BOTTOM: *Rhododendron canadense* 'Album'

TOP: *Rhododendron occidentale* 'Leonard Frisbie'
BOTTOM: *Rhododendron austrinum*

DECIDUOUS AZALEA HYBRIDS

Development of these hybrids began during the 1820s in Belgium and, as with the evergreen azaleas, has diverged into several hybrid groups. The differences among these hybrid groups are less distinct than among the evergreen types, however, because all the early deciduous hybrid groups have some parent species in common.

Eight species were used in various combinations to produce the deciduous hybrids. The American species used were *Rhododendron calendulaceum*, *R. periclymenoides* (formerly known as *R. nudiflorum*), *R. viscosum*, *R. occidentale*, and *R. arborescens*. China contributed *R. molle*, Japan *R. japonicum*, and Eurasia the notorious Pontic azalea, *R. luteum*.

The first to emerge were the Ghent hybrids, followed by the Mollis and Occidentale hybrids—all produced before 1900.

Currently there is great interest in the Knap Hill hybrids, which originated around 1870. These hybrids feature open, squarish flowers (a contribution of *R. occidentale*) in white, cream, brilliant yellow, orange, red, and all shades of pink. Breeding stock from Knap Hill varieties has given rise to various strains, of which Rothschild's Exbury strain is the most prominent.

Other hybridizers working with Knap Hill parent material have called the resulting seedlings by other names (Ilam hybrids, for example, from New Zealand) or simply designated the seedlings as their own "Knap Hill hybrids." American hybridizers have continued to produce their own hybrids both in the East and on the West Coast. These plants, mostly bred from selections of the Exbury and Knap Hill varieties, are often available in and near the areas of their origin.

Below are descriptions of the principal deciduous azalea hybrids. The code abbreviations are keyed to the variety listings that follow.

Gh—Ghent. Long considered the hardiest of azaleas until surpassed by the Northern Lights hybrids; many have survived at −25°F/−32°C. Flowers are yellow to red or pink, and generally smaller than those of the Mollis hybrids. Upright plants grow 4 to 6 feet tall.

Kn and Ex—Knap Hill and Exbury. Produce the largest flowers found on deciduous azaleas (up to 5 inches across). Hardy to about −20°F/−29°C.

Mo—Mollis. Upright plants 4 to 5 feet tall; flowers are 2½ to 4 inches wide in clusters of 7 to 13, in yellow through bright red. Hardy to −25°F/−32°C.

NL—Northern Lights. The hardiest of all deciduous azaleas, withstanding temperatures to −45°F/−43°C. Bred at the University of Minnesota from Mollis hybrids and North American species including *R. atlanticum, R. canadense,* and *R. prinophyllym.*

Oc—Occidentale. Derived from Mollis hybrids and *R. occidentale* from the Pacific states of the United States. Colors range from white flushed pink and yellow to red with orange markings. Blossoms are the size of those of

Northern Lights hybrid

the Mollis hybrids, but plants range up to 8 feet tall. Hardy to −5°F/−21°C.

Knap Hill, Exbury, and Mollis hybrids, in particular, are frequently sold as unnamed and even unbloomed seedlings. They are usually very satisfactory landscape plants because the quality of the hybrid strains is high. But for guaranteed fine flowers, your best bet is to purchase a named hybrid. If your plant is not named, buy it in bloom to be assured of its color and quality.

All deciduous azaleas need a year or more following planting or moving to re-establish themselves and resume their full blooming vigor.

BALZAC. Ex.

Fragrant, star-shaped orange red blooms, a dozen to a truss. Late May bloom.

BERRYROSE. Ex.

Fragrant, rosy salmon flowers with yellow flare. Late May bloom.

CANNON'S DOUBLE. Ex.

Cream-colored double flowers with pink petal tips. May bloom.

CECILE. Ex.

Deep pink buds opening to salmon with yellow blotch. May−early June bloom.

CENTENNIAL. See 'Washington Centennial', page 23.

FIREBALL. Kn.

Small, deep red, single flowers; bronze green foliage. May−early June bloom.

FLAMINGO. Kn.

Deep pink flowers with orange yellow blotch. Late April−May bloom.

GEORGE REYNOLDS. Ex.

Very large yellow flowers with deep gold blotch and green throat. April bloom.

GIBRALTAR. Ex.

Large, ruffled, deep orange flowers flushed red. Compact plant. Early May bloom.

GINGER. Ex.

Tight round clusters of small, bright tangerine flowers. May bloom.

GOLDEN LIGHTS. NL.

Light orange yellow flowers with deep orange yellow blotch. Hardy to −35°F/−37°C. Late May bloom.

GOLDFINCH. Kn.

Apricot flowers shaded light pink. Tall plant. Late May bloom.

HOMEBUSH. Kn.

Rose pink semidouble flowers in large, ball-shaped trusses. May bloom.

HOTSPUR RED. Ex.

Very large trusses of orange red, touched yellow on upper petals. Late May bloom.

IRENE KOSTER. Oc.

Fragrant white flowers with strong pink flush. Late May−June bloom.

KNAP HILL RED. Kn.

Small, deep red flowers; bronze foliage. Early June bloom.

KOSTER'S BRILLIANT RED. Mo.

Brilliant orange red flowers. Early June bloom.

LEMONORA. Mo.

Medium yellow flowers touched with pink. Tall plant. Late May bloom.

MY MARY.

Bred from native American species. Fragrant, pure yellow flowers in round clusters on plants of moderate height (3 to 4 feet tall). Late May bloom.

OLD GOLD. Ex.

Light orange yellow flowers, flushed pink, with deep orange blotch. Late May bloom.

ORCHID LIGHTS. NL.

Purplish pink flowers with yellow spotting. Exceptional hardiness (to −45°F/−43°C) comes from its *R. canadense* parent. Late May bloom.

OXYDOL. Ex.

🦋 Very large white flowers with large yellow blotch in throat. Free-flowering plant with bronzy leaves. April bloom.

PEACHY KEEN. Ilam.

🦋 Light pink flowers touched with red. Compact plant. May bloom.

PRINCESS ROYAL. Ex.

🦋🦋 Pink buds opening to huge, fragrant, ivory blooms with pink flush. May bloom.

RENNE. Ex.

🦋 Deep red flowers suffused yellow. Early May bloom.

TOP: 'Gibraltar'
BOTTOM: 'Irene Koster' with *Scilla siberica*

ROSE RUFFLES. Ex.

🦋 Ruffled rose pink flowers. Extremely floriferous. Late May–June bloom.

ROSY LIGHTS. NL.

🦋 Purplish pink flowers with reddish orange spotting. Plant is hardy to −45°F/−43°C. Late May bloom.

SNOWBIRD.

🦋 Natural hybrid between *R. atlanticum* and *R. canescens*. The 4- to 6-foot-tall shrub produces masses of fragrant, pure white flowers. April–May bloom.

SPICY LIGHTS. NL.

🦋 Large clusters of light salmon orange flowers with orange yellow blotch. Hardy to −35°F/−37°C. May bloom.

STRAWBERRY ICE. Ex.

🦋 Frilled trusses of coral pink flowers with yellow blotch on upper petals. May bloom.

SUN CHARIOT. Ex.

🦋 Soft apricot yellow flowers on a compact, spreading plant. May bloom.

SYLPHIDES. Kn.

🦋 Very light pink flowers with yellow shading in the center. Late May bloom.

TUTTI FRUTTI. Ex.

🦋 Rose-colored blooms with large red blotch on the upper petals. Late April–May bloom.

WASHINGTON CENTENNIAL.

🦋🦋 A hybrid of *R. occidentale*. Large frilled flowers opening light orange yellow and changing to pale pink to white; the uppermost petal is bright yellow. Fragrant. May bloom.

TOP: 'My Mary'
CENTER: 'Old Gold'
BOTTOM: 'Orchid Lights'

WHITE LIGHTS. NL.

🦋 Pink buds opening to paler pink to white flowers. Hardy to −35°F/−37°C. May–June bloom

WHITETHROAT. Kn.

🦋 Small, fragrant, pure white double flowers. Profuse late May bloom.

WINDSOR BUTTERCUP. Ex.

🦋 Selected from Exbury hybrids grown at Windsor Great Park in England. Round trusses of brilliant daffodil yellow flowers on a compact plant. May bloom.

RH

INTRODUCING

RHODODENDRONS

While almost everyone knows of the rhododendron, few are aware of the great diversity that exists in this family. Plants range in size from minute trailers to 80-foot forest trees. Flowers of most are carried in rounded or pyramidal clusters at the branch ends and are generally large and attractive. Colors range from white and yellow through pink to rosy red, scarlet, nearly azure blue, and purple.

The foliage of the evergreen kinds is also attractive. In fact, few hardy shrubs can match the rhododendron in being equally blessed in foliage and flower. This quality gives them year-round beauty, with no "down time" except for the brief period when the blossoms fade. Although their shape and size can be controlled, they do not need routine yearly pruning. Most are substantial plants that make significant contributions to the landscape, either near the house as foundation plants, as focal points in the shrub border, or massed along drives or at the woodland edge.

An additional blessing, to the gardener who regards Latin or scientific names as an onerous and unnecessary burden, is the fact that Latin and common names are the same.

Rhododendrons and pink dogwood put on a show behind low-blooming azaleas in spring. Sword ferns and lily-of-the-valley grow between borders.

Massed rhododendrons and azaleas thrive in sunlight filtered by overhead trees.

WHAT IS A RHODODENDRON?

Rhododendrons are shrubs or trees in the heath family (Ericaceae). *Most are evergreen, but some very conspicuous exceptions are deciduous. The genus is large, including perhaps 900 species, and the number keeps climbing with continued exploration. There are countless hybrids.*

The name "rhododendron" is derived from Greek words meaning rose tree. *It was the Swedish botanist Linnaeus who, in systematizing the chaotic world of plant names in the 18th century, first used the name to identify* Rhododendron ponticum, *a purple-flowering shrub native to the Caucasus and other parts of the eastern and western Mediterranean. (Some earlier writers had conferred the name "rhododendron" on the oleander.)*

Several botanists have attempted to impose order on this huge and varied genus by dividing it into subgenera, each containing several sections, which in turn are divided into subsections. These technicalities are of little interest to the general gardener, although they're fascinating to taxonomists and hybridizers. The subgenus *Rhododendron* embraces the plants we call rhododendrons; almost all are evergreen, although a few from the near-Arctic regions and the highest mountains are deciduous. The subgenera *Pentanthera* (deciduous azaleas) and *Tsutsusi* (evergreen azaleas) are described in Chapter 1, "Introducing Azaleas," beginning on page 4.

Like nearly all plants in the heath family, rhododendrons like acid soil. Most originate from woodland regions where soil is rich in humus and heavy rainfall leaches away any calcium that might tip the soil pH toward alkalinity. With few exceptions, they love the humidity and cool air of the mountains (some thrive at sea level in temperate climates). Many of the dwarf sorts grow in thin, rocky soil at high elevations. A few family members even grow in the tundra above the Arctic Circle, and a large number in warm, temperate, or tropical regions grow in moss or plant debris in trees or on rocks.

RHODODENDRONS IN THE WILD

To see the many species of rhododendron in their native habitat would require a long and exciting journey. The place to begin would be the mountainous region where India, Burma, and

China meet, generally considered the ancestral home of the genus. Certainly the greatest number of species is found here.

Let's visit an imaginary location on the northeastern frontier of Burma. At the lower elevations (up to 8,000 feet), rhododendrons are few and inconspicuous. A thousand feet higher, you may smell rhododendrons before you see them; unable to compete for light and nourishment in the dense rain forest, they flaunt their Easter lily flowers high on trees or rocks as epiphytes. The only visible evidence of them may be blossoms that fall to the forest floor, or a glimpse of white or pink high in the crotch of a tree. Specimens of these tender species must be grown in greenhouses except in the mildest, coolest regions, such as the Northern California coast, Ireland, the west of England, and the cooler parts of New Zealand's North Island.

At the same elevation or a bit higher, we may find that we're walking *under* a rhododendron; the first tree-size rhododendrons we encounter will appear in this constantly moist rain forest. Climbing another thousand feet or so, we come to the heart of the temperate rain forest, where a number of familiar trees are growing—evergreen oaks, magnolias, maples, and a scattering of tree rhododendrons. Where sufficient light is available (on rocky ledges, for instance), a host of shrubby rhododendrons may be seen.

Eventually, as we continue the upward climb, we find broad-leafed trees giving way to conifers, especially firs. Among them are thickets and groves of rhododendrons: gnarled treelike examples, scrubby types growing amid bamboo thickets, and picturesque plants literally hanging from crevices in the cliffs or cascading over rocks. Early spring brings on a breathtaking spectacle of light green and bronzy new foliage, dark bluish green fir trees, and everywhere frothy billows of rhododendron flowers in scarlet, white, pink, lemon, and purple.

Even above the timberline, rhododendron thickets 2 to 3 feet high persist, so dense in growth that walking is made difficult. Finally, in the highest moorlands—where summers are dry, sunshine is intense, and the ground is covered by snow 6 months of the year—hundreds of square miles of calf-high rhododendrons clothe the rocks and meadows with blossoms of pink, purple, amber, or gold.

By making several such journeys in the first half of the 20th century and closely studying these rhododendrons in their native habitat, plant explorer Frank Kingdon Ward determined that the more congenial a climate is for rhododendrons, the greater will be the number of species growing there—though the range of each may be small. The tremendous heights of these Burmese mountain ranges and the deep gorges separating them isolate many species and restrict them to a narrow range.

Farther north in China, gentler terrain permits the broader spread of species, and increasing latitude makes for hardier plants. Many shrubby rhododendrons found here have been important in the breeding of modern garden rhododendrons. In the extreme north of China, Manchuria, and eastern Siberia, a few hardy rhododendrons persist, and one, the dwarf *R. lapponicum*, crosses to Alaska and northern Scandinavia. Japan's moist, temperate climate supports a number of species, including many evergreen azaleas.

To the west, the Asiatic rhododendrons extend through Afghanistan and, with Linnaeus's *R. ponticum*, to the Caucasus Mountains and beyond to Portugal and Spain.

In the Western Hemisphere, Oregon, Washington, and California host three species, while the eastern United States supports many more. The greatest concentration can be

TOP: Mixed rhododendrons line a garden path.

BOTTOM: The spring blooms of a rhododendron and a cherry complement each other.

found in the Appalachian Mountains, where *R. maximum* may form thickets many acres in extent and *R. catawbiense*, the ancestor of most of our hardiest rhododendrons, paints the glades at higher elevations with its purple flowers. Here and at lower elevations extending southward to Florida and westward to Texas also grow many species of deciduous azaleas.

The second greatest concentration of rhododendron species grows in the tropics of Southeast Asia. The Vireyas, or Malesian, rhododendrons grow from Taiwan and the Philippines through the Malay Peninsula and the islands of Indonesia to New Guinea, where the largest number is to be found. The southern-most species grows in the rain forest of northern Queensland, in Australia. For more on this rather little known group, see "Vireyas" on page 105.

'Pink Pearl'

RHODODENDRONS THEN AND NOW

TOP: *Rhododendron catawbiense*
BOTTOM: *Rhododendron maximum*

The English were the first to collect wild rhododendrons for introduction into gardens. Although the earliest rhododendron to reach England arrived from the Alps in 1656, the next four did not arrive until 80 years later—this time from the American colonies.

During the rest of the 1700s, an additional seven species came into cultivation, including, for the first time, some northern Asiatic species raised from seed sent to England by the German naturalist Pallas. Early in the 1800s, a few more new species reached English gardens—among them two that would spark the explosion of rhododendron hybrids.

The first, the American *R. catawbiense*, which decorates the southern Appalachian mountains with its globes of pink, mauve, and lavender, arrived in England from North Carolina in 1809. Color purists today criticize the amount of blue in the pink flowers, but they don't deny that the Catawba rhododendron produces blooms in large, showy, compact trusses—and, most

significant—on very hardy, adaptable, compact shrubs. This species and some of its varieties are still widely sold where hardiness to cold is important.

The pioneer British hybridizer Michael Waterer anticipated the Catawba's value the year after its introduction and crossed it with the other large native of the eastern United States, *R. maximum*. His was the first careful attempt to guide rhododendron evolution. A similar hybrid, 'Maxecat', is still sold.

The other species to ignite the imagination of the rhododendron enthusiasts was *R. arboreum*, a Himalayan tree sent to England in 1811. It was the first southeast Asiatic species to grow in English gardens. Fourteen years after its introduction, the first plants flowered—in dazzling scarlet.

Up until this time, rhododendrons had caused little excitement among gardeners. The taste of the time was formal, and clipped boxwood, laurel, and yew were the plants of choice. The development of a freer, more natural style in garden design coincided with the appearance of the new hybrids.

EAST MEETS WEST

Because the spectacular *R. arboreum* was too tender for all but the very mildest coastal English gardens, several hybridizers attempted to combine its blazing red color with hardier plants, including the Catawba rhododendron and several of its early hybrids. Their efforts resulted in hybrids with deep pink and red flowers; some of these are still grown today.

The real importance of the first British hybrids of Asiatic species, however, was that they suggested possibilities that might lie ahead. Even in the first-generation seedlings from *R. arboreum*, hybridizers captured much of the color they wanted on plants that could endure more severe winter cold.

The excitement generated by these hybrids sent plant explorers into British India to seek out more exotic species to put into the hybridists' hands. The notable explorer Sir Joseph Hooker, for example, scouted the small Himalayan kingdom of Sikkim and in 1850 sent to England 45 new species, which he described and illustrated handsomely in *Rhododendrons of the Sikkim Himalaya.*

Throughout the rest of the century, more new species were discovered and introduced, mostly from Asia; by 1900 some 300 were in cultivation. It was also during the latter part of the 19th century that extensive breeding programs produced a number of hybrids that even today are recommended (in areas where they are hardy) as reliable, attractive garden rhododendrons—'Cynthia', 'Pink Pearl', 'Purple Splendour', and 'Sappho', to name just a few.

THE 20TH-CENTURY POPULATION EXPLOSION

With 300 species and numerous hybrids available at the turn of the century, it appeared that gardeners and hybridizers had at their disposal more than enough material to satisfy their horticultural and experimental desires. Few would have imagined that during the first three decades of the 1900s, plant-hunting expeditions would nearly triple the number of available species.

The first plant explorer to make significant collections in western China was Ernest H. ("Chinese") Wilson. Hired by an English nursery to search for the fabled dove tree *(Davidia),* he encountered an amazing variety of new plants—rhododendrons among them—in the provinces of western China. Wilson sent back from his first expedition nearly as many new species as Hooker had 50 years earlier, and his three subsequent expeditions were nearly as fruitful as the first.

Other courageous, dedicated, determined men in the employ of various nurseries, arboretums, foundations, and consortiums of rich collectors made their mark through the quantity and quality of their new discoveries. Joseph Rock, whom some older readers may recall from his many articles in *National Geographic,* collected in western China and Tibet, risking his life at the hands of bandits and warlike Tibetan monks. Many of his rhododendron introductions still grow in the University of California Botanical Garden in Berkeley.

Reginald Farrer wrote in jeweled prose of his explorations in northwestern China and the boundaries of Tibet. And Frank Kingdon Ward had the thrill of being the first westerner to glimpse a miles-high moorland in western China covered with alpine rhododendrons in "a chromatic storm-tossed surf—rose, pink, lavender, purple, and amber—through which one may wade ankle deep for days on end."

HYBRIDS AND HYBRIDIZERS

The reputation of rhododendrons as a rich man's flower has some basis, but not because rhododendrons are so difficult to grow or so initially expensive that only the wealthy can afford them. Rather, among private gardeners in the 19th and early 20th centuries, it was wealthy and titled persons who had the time to

devote to growing these plants and the land on which to do it, since most of the early rhododendron hybrids and their parent species were large shrubs. They also had the money to support the garden staff necessary to look after large collections.

Probably the most remarkable such person was the late Lionel de Rothschild, who assembled the world's largest (and possibly finest) rhododendron collection at his Exbury estate on England's south coast between 1920 and 1942. Exbury's greenhouses were built with bronze from its own foundry and teak from its own sawmill. Rothschild's weekend guests were given brushes and pollen and sent forth to hybridize plants he had selected and to record the crosses. On Monday morning he would motor back to London and fix the price of gold. With the

Exbury Gardens, Lionel de Rothschild's estate on England's south coast

best resources at his disposal and guided by impeccable taste, he produced numerous hybrids outstanding for their refinement and quality. Exbury still exists as a garden and as a public nursery.

During the same period, the United States had a gifted amateur hybridizer in Charles Dexter, of Sandwich, Massachusetts. Using native hardy rhododendrons and hybrids and a wide variety of more tender kinds, he made many crosses of very high quality and considerable hardiness. Although he kept few records and named few plants, he distributed thousands of his hybrids. Many of them may be seen today at the Heritage Foundation in Sandwich, at the base of Cape Cod.

Gifted amateurs produced many beautiful hybrids, but professional nurserymen were responsible for the vast bulk that were generally available to gardeners. In listings of standard hybrids, the nursery names Waterer and Slocock in England and Koster and van Nes in Holland appear again and again. Because the concerns of these companies were commercial as well as aesthetic, they emphasized commercial advantages as much as beauty in their hybrids. They produced rhododendrons that were easy to propagate and quick to grow to salable size, with sturdy, attractive plants; vigorous, trouble-free growth; and large flowers in compact trusses.

TOMORROW'S RHODODENDRONS

These might better be described as the rhododendrons of today and tomorrow. New varieties once reached consumers slowly, increase being limited by the amount of wood available for cuttings. Tissue culture has made the rapid multiplication of new varieties practical, and as a result the span between first bloom and appearance in nurseries has greatly narrowed.

As gardeners discover the increasing variety of colors, forms, sizes, and foliage qualities available, and become familiar with basic cultural guidelines, the popularity of rhododendrons is bound to increase. Three particular trends in development promise to promote that popularity.

EMPHASIS ON SMALLER PLANTS. The discovery of many new Asiatic rhododendrons during the first three decades of this century opened up possibilities for colors, plant forms, and flower cluster forms beyond the familiar English and Dutch hybrids. The flood of new species included not only alpine dwarfs and forest giants, but also species of small to intermediate size—with smaller leaves than the typical nursery hybrids and with flowers in informal clusters. These species have been taken in hand by a number of contemporary hybridizers intent on developing smaller plants that will fit more comfortably into the ever-shrinking suburban garden.

Notable among these species is *R. yakushimanum (R. degronianum yakushimanum)*. This plant combines all the classic features of a rhododendron—large, glossy leaves and good-size round clusters of flowers at the branch ends—in a small (1- to 4-foot), compact plant. These virtues, combined with hardiness and attractive white-furred new growth and thick brown felt beneath the leaves, have made the "yaks" and their hybrids highly favored plants.

Among other rhododendron species being used to reduce plant size to acceptable suburban standards are *R. forrestii repens,* a creeping plant with scarlet flowers, and *R.*

Rhododendron yakushimanum surrounds a garden gazebo.

keiskei, a 2-foot Japanese shrub with yellow flowers.

BETTER PLANTS FROM BETTER PARENTS. Continued exploration and the extensive culture of species from seed have shown how variable most species are, and how important it is to use fine, selected forms in hybridizing programs. The nursery trade now offers superior selections of many species (*R. yakushimanum* 'Koichiro Wada' or *R. y.* 'Yaku Angel', for instance) that flower more freely, have better color, or have better plant form than run-of-the mill seedlings.

A classic example of the value of good parent material is the superb assemblage of named hybrids in the Loderi group. Their originator, Sir Edmund Loder, carefully chose the best forms of *R. griffithianum* and *R. fortunei* and produced from them, around 1901, a number of hybrids still unsurpassed for floral magnificence.

EXTENSION OF GROWING RANGE. With research, breeding, and dauntless experimentation by gardeners, the growing of rhododendrons has been extended to areas once thought unsuitable. Home gardeners have discovered by trial and error that many varieties will thrive under conditions generally described as inhospitable. The growth in the popularity of rhododendrons in the southern United States—where soil fungi were thought to be the limiting factor—is proof that presumed obstacles can be overcome. Similarly, better knowledge of how to manage problems arising from heat, soil alkalinity, and poor-quality water makes it possible for gardeners in California's central valley to enjoy rhododendrons as permanent landscape plants.

The dedicated efforts of amateurs and professional growers have been indispensable in developing new varieties that will perform in regions too cold, hot, or dry for the greater number of available hybrids. For every 'Scintillation', 'Catalgla', or 'PJM' that will survive −25°F/−32°C winter temperatures, hundreds of thousands of seedlings must be planted and subjected to the trial of climate. The results, however, have been spectacular, and newer hybrids are rapidly becoming available to home gardeners each year.

TOP: *R. yakushimanum* 'CHP'
BOTTOM: *R. yakushimanum* 'Yaku Angel'

RHODODENDRON COUNTRY

Rhododendron culture is easiest in regions where you find native species. Even though such areas won't be ideal for all types, you can be sure of a basic "rightness" of soil, atmosphere, and moisture that will favor at least some rhododendrons with a minimum of care. One basic limiting factor in choice of varieties is winter cold: the temperate environment of, say, San Francisco, allows a much wider choice than you'd have in the more bracing climates of Boston and Cleveland—or even Seattle and Vancouver.

The darker shaded portions of the map show terrain that rhododendrons naturally take to—country with high rainfall or high humidity, acid soil, and free drainage on slopes. The Pacific Northwest is rhododendron paradise. The California coastal fog belt grows most rhododendrons with ease, and is the only place where many frost-tender kinds survive. The inland valleys of the Pacific states pose a heat problem, but many rhododendrons survive there if given adequate drainage, shade, and water. A few rhododendrons have been grown in Southern California, but only 'Anah Kruschke' can be considered a success, although some growers have succeeded with the tropical Vireyas (see page 105).

In the East, winter cold sets the northern limits for rhododendrons, while heat combined with humidity limits success in the South. The lightly shaded areas of the map show where careful growers can succeed with some of the more cold- and heat-tolerant species and varieties. Breeders here and abroad are working to push the limits of cold and heat tolerance. In the High Plains, summer heat, winter cold and wind, and unfavorable soil make it exceedingly difficult to grow rhododendrons, but Denver has achieved some success with the ironclads (see page 34).

The further you are from rhodendrons' "natural" territory, the closer attention you must pay to the plants' basic needs. If you wish to experiment with rhododendrons in less-than-ideal climates, start with the ironclad hybrids of *Rhododendron catawbiense:* The old Catawba hybrids are not just generally the most cold tolerant; they're also quite rugged overall—able to withstand heat, dry air, cold, and unfavorable soil. Many of the lepidote rhododendrons are also quite cold-tolerant. Wherever you live, look before you leap: inquire at local botanical gardens, cooperative extension services, and the best local nurseries to find out your chances for success.

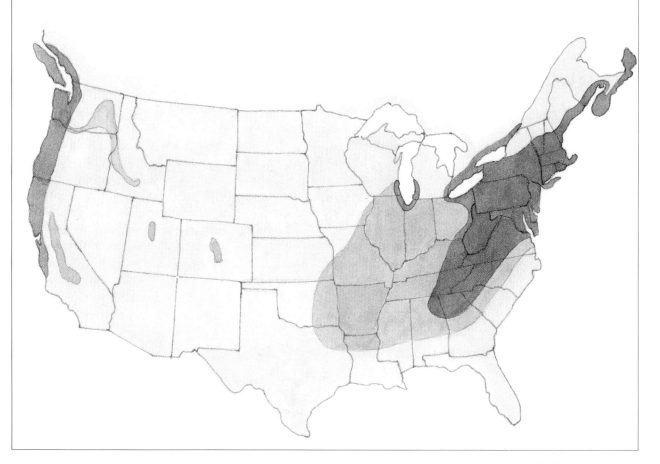

Low-growing rhododendrons and smooth,
bluish boulders edge a small pond.

RHODODENDRONS IN THE LANDSCAPE

New rhododendron enthusiasts often think of these plants simply as compact, heavily foliaged shrubs that bear rounded trusses of large flowers—typical of the English and Dutch nursery hybrids that grace many a public park. The differences between one rhododendron and another may seem no greater than the differences between modern hybrid tea rose varieties.

With greater exposure to rhododendrons, however, comes the thrilling revelation of how great the variety in growth and foliage is—from ground cover shrublets with narrow leaves to large-leafed tree types—not to mention the nearly complete range of colors—omitting only pure azure blue (although some come close) and black (again, some come close).

Considering the variation in growth types alone, rhododendrons have nearly limitless landscape uses as long as growing conditions are favorable. There are rhododendrons you can use as you would floribunda roses—as low hedges to divide garden areas and as foreground border plants. The dwarf types are naturals for rock gardens. Those with lanky, pliable growth are effective when trained as espaliers on trellises or against protected walls. Larger sorts are admirably suited to serve as background shrubs in wide plantings and as screening shrubs.

CREATING A WOODLAND GARDEN

Azaleas, rhododendrons, and dogwood create
overlapping layers of spring blossoms.

The rhododendron setting *par excellence* is, of course, the woodland garden. Lionel de Rothschild is reputed to have said that no garden, however small, should be without its acre of wild woodland. This may seem a bitter joke to the urban gardener, but a semblance of such a garden is practical for those who live in the country or the outer suburbs. Rothschild's own wild woodland was considerably civilized by the addition of thousands of rhododendrons and azaleas, and any fortunate possessor of a small woodlot can approximate Rothschild's property by adding more modest quantities of these shrubs. Complementary plantings of flowering trees such as cherry, crabapple, dogwood, and goldenchain *(Laburnum)*, and shade-loving ground covers (anemones, trilliums, and a host of other plants) would create a garden rich in beauty and variety.

The tree cover shouldn't be too dense; rhododendrons grow lanky and bloom sparsely under such conditions. A grove of well-spaced trees with high-branching limbs provides best light. The shelter of trees also will make several degrees' difference in the soil temperature, preventing overheating in summer and helping retain heat in winter. The overhead protection is especially helpful with plants of borderline hardiness, as it will slow spring growth and lessen the danger of late frost to early-breaking leaves or flower buds.

Open oak woodlands are splendid places to grow rhododendrons; the oak leaves decompose slowly, providing a long-lasting mulch. Deciduous woodlands also offer a summer background, while in winter the rhododendron foliage relieves the woodlands' bare-branched look. Try to avoid planting beneath trees with heavy shade and greedy roots, such as ash, beech, elm, the larger maples, magnolia, poplar, pin oak, and sycamore.

If not too dense, coniferous trees offer good shade, and the fallen needles provide a first-rate mulch. As a general rule, set rhododendrons at least 5 to 6 feet from the tree trunks. Such trees often have a dense network of surface roots that extend for some distance from the trunk. These can deprive the rhododendrons of food and water.

Even if you don't own a woodlot, you can show rhododendrons to great advantage if your property abuts a forest, as many do in the Northwest and New England. A coniferous forest is the finest background for rhododendron plantings, and if the forest contains color relief in the form of dogwood or shadblow *(Amelanchier),* so much the better.

APPRECIATING RHODODENDRON FOLIAGE

When shopping for rhododendrons, many gardeners are so dazzled by the blossoms that they fail to notice the variety of foliage colors and finishes, which can be nearly as important in the

'Northern Starburst' combines with hellebores.

landscape as any floral display. Just a little browsing will disclose a wide range of greens—from light to very dark, or even gray or blue, and with glossy to soft matte finishes. With thoughtfully chosen background and companion plantings, such rhododendrons can be like jewels in an expensive setting, both in and out of bloom. The size range of rhododendron leaves is also immense, from ½ inch in some of the dwarf species to well over 2 feet in some of the treelike species. The latter produce an effect that approaches the truly tropical.

A number of rhododendrons have another feature that can be exploited by the clever gardener. On some species and their hybrids, the undersides of the leaves are covered with a dense covering of short hairs like peach fuzz called *indumentum.* Often orange, bronze, or silver in color, the indumentum contrasts handsomely with the green upper leaf surface. If these rhododendrons are located where you can look up at the plant and see the undersides of the leaves, the effect can be striking.

Some rhododendrons also produce new growth in orange, red, bronze, white, or chocolate hues that rival any floral display. With increased familiarity, you'll find rhododendrons so attractive in foliage and plant form that you'd cherish them even if they never bloomed.

EXTENDING THE SEASON

Most nurseries that carry just a few rhododendrons offer the time-tested English and Dutch nursery hybrids, all of which come into glorious bloom at about the same time. A wider plant search will turn up early- and late-blooming species and varieties that will stretch the blooming season from January to September in mild climates, March to July where winters are more severe, and even throughout the year with species and varieties in the Vireya section.

Not only can you keep a particular garden vista in flower for several months by interplanting rhododendrons with different bloom seasons, but you can even control the mood of your planting throughout the total bloom season: the earliest display might feature yellow, orange, cream, and salmon colors; that could be followed by a show of reds, pinks, and blush whites; and the last burst might contain lavenders, purples, violets, and cream colors.

CHOOSE PLANTS WITH MATURE SIZE IN MIND

In small gardens, rhododendrons are used principally as foundation shrubs. Consider carefully the ultimate size of each rhododendron you select and the length of time it will take to attain that size. Sizes listed for rhododendrons are based on height and spread at 10 years. Most will continue to grow after that time, and although size can be controlled by pruning, and rhododendrons are easy to move, you can avoid needless labor by careful selection and placement. Too many windows have vanished behind foreground plantings, and too many potentially shapely specimen plants have been turned into grotesque parodies by overcrowding and competition for space. Give your plants enough room to grow.

IRONCLAD RHODODENDRONS

'Nova Zembla'

"Ironclad" is the term applied to the rhododendrons that are hardiest to cold—the ones most likely to survive low winter temperatures at the extreme northern and western boundaries of "Rhododendron Country." By luck, many of these plants are also among the most tolerant of high summer temperatures. They won't thrive in the notoriously cold winters of Cut Bank or West Yellowstone, Montana, nor in hot spots like Yuma, Arizona, and Del Rio, Texas, but they're the rhododendrons beloved by New Englanders, southerners, and people from the plains. What's the secret of their toughness?

It isn't that they come from the coldest places on earth. There are rhododendrons in Siberia and Alaska, and any number of species growing high in the Himalayas, but they don't look the way we expect rhododendrons to look, nor can we give them growing conditions they need to survive in our gardens. They're covered with snow much of the year, and during their brief summers they experience either very long days or the intense sunlight of high peaks.

The secret to temperature tolerance within our gardens lies with a few species that come from regions with marked differences in winter and summer temperatures—eastern North America and northeastern Asia.

Most important among the ancestors of these ironclads is the Catawba rhododendron, *R. catawbiense*, native to the mountains of Virginia and North Carolina, where both winter and summer temperatures may be extreme. Many ironclads are simple selections from the wild population of the Catawba rhododendron. Most are the result of hybrids within this species. Less important as a parent (because of its great size, small flower trusses, and late bloom season) but even hardier is *R. maximum*, which grows from eastern Canada to Georgia.

Another eastern American parent is *R. minus* or *R. carolinianum*, a smaller plant native to the southeastern states. It and *R. dauricum*—a very hardy purple-flowered shrub from Mongolia, northern China, eastern Siberia, and Japan—are the parents of numerous offspring of small-leafed, small-flowered hybrids that bloom very early.

Rhododendron specialists from prime rhododendron country in Northern California and the Northwest tend to look down on these plants for the lack of purity of their bluish reds (or reddish purples), but the ironclads are still widely planted there for their toughness, heat tolerance, and ease of culture. They will thrive if any rhododendron will. Elsewhere in the country they're still the most widely planted rhododendrons. Moreover, their virtues are being incorporated into newer hybrids with a wider range of clearer colors, which, though not quite so hardy, are suited to all but the very coldest gardens.

Here are some of the real ironclads, hardy to −25° F/−32°C. All are large-flowered plants with *R. catawbiense*, *R. maximum*, or both in their ancestry.

White: 'Boule de Neige', 'Catalgla', 'Catawbiense Album'
Pink: 'English Rosuem', 'Maxecat', 'Roseum Elegans'
Red: 'Henry's Red', 'Nova Zembla'
Lavender or Purple: 'Catawbiense Boursault', 'President Roosevelt'

The following lepidotes (scaly-leafed rhododendrons) have smaller leaves and smaller flower thant those above, but they bloom profusely:

'Northern Starburst'. An improved 'PJM' Manitou. White aging to pink
'PJM'. Strong purplish pink
'PJM Compact'. Smaller than 'PJM'
'PJM Elite'. Deeper color than 'PJM'
'PJM Regal'. Ealier bloom than 'PJM'
'Ramapo'. Violet flowers on a dwarf plant

Using smaller rhododendrons

Seduced by the stately form and impressive flowers of the standard rhododendrons, some gardeners may overlook a host of smaller-growing species and varieties that would be appropriate even in tiny urban gardens. These may be smaller versions of their large-leafed cousins; true dwarfs with reduced leaf, plant, and flower size; miniature densely twiggy plants with small leaves and flowers; or even prostrate kinds that trail over rocks in their native habitat. The larger of these may be planted in front of or between their big cousins, or used as foundation plants around low, sprawling houses. The densely twiggy sorts (*R. impeditum*, for instance) are useful low ground covers on well-drained sites. They're also choice bonsai subjects in that, like Kurume azaleas, they possess a free-branching, twiggy growth habit, small leaves, and modest-sized flowers. The prostrate or low mounding types are excellent rock garden plants.

Growing rhododendrons in containers

The fibrous, shallow root systems of rhododendrons make these plants fine subjects for container planting. Where soil conditions or natural shade is lacking, container culture may be the best way to enjoy rhododendrons: it allows gardeners to give plants the proper soil mix, control feeding and watering, and move them about to take advantage of shade from trees, an overhead lattice, or walls and fences. Although rhododendrons are attractive even without flowers, those who insist on maximum performance from the garden may replace out-of-bloom rhododendrons with pots containing roses, hibiscus, or mixed annuals or perennials.

In addition, adventuresome gardeners might wish to grow rhododendrons that aren't quite hardy in their regions. Container-grown plants can be sheltered against the coldest weather by bringing them into a glassed-in porch, an unheated (or barely heated) greenhouse, or (for short periods only) a garage or cellar. The Vireya rhododendrons are an example in point: they *must* be grown in containers and treated as house plants in all but the very mildest climates.

For more information on container culture for rhododendrons, see "Growing in Containers" on page 97.

Companion plants

It's possible to landscape with rhododendrons alone (at least in the most favored climates), but most landscapes are more varied and interesting with other plants as companions. Among the many compatible companions are rhododendron relatives from the heath family, notably mountain laurel *(Kalmia latifolia)*, *Enkianthus*, *Leucothoe*, and *Pieris*. Where heath and heather *(Erica* and *Calluna)* aren't too rambunctious, they make good foreground plantings for rhododendrons growing in the sun.

Many other shrubs also thrive under the conditions that favor rhododendrons, among them camellia, *Corylopsis*, *Fothergilla*, *Hydrangea*, *Osmanthus delavayi*, skimmia, and many viburnums. To be suitable as ground covers near rhododendrons, plants shouldn't be too vigorous; ajuga is satisfactory, as are wild ginger *(Asarum)*, golden star *(Chrysogonum)*, and some ferns. Perennials with attractive flowers are too numerous to list, but anemone, *Astilbe*, hellebore, hosta, toad lily *(Tricyrtis)*, and trillium are first-rate selections.

Favored trees include Japanese maple, dogwood (select anthracnose-resistant varieties where the disease is a problem), *Franklinia*, katsura tree *(Cercidiphyllum)*, *Parrotia persica*, *Stewartia*, *Styrax*, sourwood or sorrel tree *(Oxydendrum)*, and silver bell *(Halesia)*.

TOP: White rhododendrons flank steps and terrace.

BOTTOM: Rhododendrons, white candytuft, and basket-of-gold bloom together in a Northwest garden.

A SPECIAL CAUTION FOR CALIFORNIA GARDENS

In California, many gardens have inherited large native oaks. The shade these provide is tempting to the rhododendron fancier, but rhododendrons—or any other water-loving plants, for that matter—should never be planted near these trees. Heavy summer irrigation will promote the growth of fungi in the warm soil and cause rot where the oak trunk emerges from the soil, destroying the bark, the cambium layer, and eventually the tree. Plant out near the drip line or beyond.

RHODODENDRON SHOWCASE

Shopping for rhododendrons can be, literally, a beautiful experience. But it can also be somewhat bewildering if you're confronted with an assortment of varieties about which you know nothing. The listings on the next pages include the most popular and widely grown varieties, giving descriptions of plants and flowers, sizes, bloom seasons, and hardiness. The following paragraphs clarify the abbreviated information given in the listings.

TOP: 'Nova Zembla'
CENTER: 'Summer Summit'
BOTTOM: 'Trude Webster'

PLANT SIZE AT MATURITY. The American Rhododendron Society (ARS) uses average plant height at 10 years of age as the basis for this figure. Plants can grow taller as they pass the 10-year mark, but size can be controlled by pinching or pruning (see pages 90–96). Low plants (to 3 feet or less) are usually slow growing and unlikely to exceed the 10-year height by much.

HARDINESS RATINGS. Disappointed by discrepancies between several hardiness ratings of hybrids by the British Rhododendron Society and the performance in this country of the rated plants, the ARS set out to re-evaluate hybrid and species temperature tolerances. The new ratings are still undergoing some modification as plants are subjected to unusual conditions. When reading the published hardiness ratings, remember that local conditions (especially in hilly and mountainous areas) may vary considerably; gardens at lower elevations usually experience lower temperatures. The timing of low temperatures can also determine a plant's sensitivity to cold: cold spells that follow warm weather or that strike after growth has started can damage a plant even though temperatures stay within the plant's rated hardiness. Wind, winter sunshine during cold weather, and dehydration caused by the plant's inability to replace transpired moisture from frozen soil may be more damaging than extreme low temperatures.

SEASON OF BLOOM. The following abbreviations are used in the listings to indicate season of bloom: VE—Very Early; E—Early; EM—Early–Midseason; M—Midseason; ML— Midseason–Late; L—Late; VL—Very Late.

These bloom seasons are relative to your climate, of course. In milder climates, bloom may extend over 5 months, with earliest varieties flowering in February and the latest in June or July. In colder parts of "Rhododendron Country" (see page 31), the bloom season will be shorter and will begin later.

RHODODENDRON QUALITY RATINGS. Some years ago the British Rhododendron Society initiated a system of rating the quality of hybrids and species. From one to four stars indicated increasing quality; a no-star rating denoted either a very poor sort or a hybrid too new or unexceptional to be rated. Beginning in 1950, the ARS established a rating system to be based on evaluations made in the United States. Expressed either as numerals or corresponding numbers of plus marks, the ratings are 5—Superior; 4—Above average; 3—Average; 2—Below average; 1—Poor.

Using the number system, a variety may be rated for flower quality, plant appearance, and plant performance, in that order. Thus, a rating of 5/3/3 tells you the bloom is "Superior" on a plant of "Average" attractiveness and "Average" performance in the garden. You may notice that at times one of these ratings will be split between two numbers. A 4–5/3/3 rating means that the flower quality has been variously assessed as being "Above average" or "Superior," while plant appearance and performance have both received "Average" ratings. A rating of 4/4/3–2 means that the plant is "Above average" in bloom and plant appearance, but "Average" or "Below average" in plant performance. "Unrated" may mean the variety is too new to be rated or simply not registered with the ARS. It is tempting to shop for plants with the highest flower rating, but be sure to note hardiness, size, and performance as well.

In considering these ratings, consider also where you garden. A rhododendron must live and thrive in your garden to be worth growing. If you don't live in an ideal rhododendron climate, you won't be able to grow some of the most highly rated varieties; however, you'll still derive much pleasure from the varieties you can grow.

A FEW SPECIAL TERMS

The botanical world has its own dictionary of terms—words that take on special meanings when used in connection with plants, and words especially coined for talking about plants. Here are some terms that you'll encounter in the descriptive listings.

GROUP (grex). All seedlings resulting from a cross between two different rhododendrons or any subsequent crosses between the same parents, indicated in the following listings by a "g." after a plant name (for example, Fabia g.). Such plants share many characteristics but differ in some aspect, such as color, form or markings. Nurseries may sell any seedling from the cross with the group name, so if you buy Fabia, for instance, you're not getting a particular plant, just a particular ancestry. Varieties, selected forms propagated by cuttings or grafting, are given individual names, such as 'Fabia Tangerine'.

HYBRID. Any rhododendron that has resulted from cross-fertilization of two other rhododendrons. Hybrids may have been planned or produced by a hybridizer or may have occurred spontaneously in the wild (in the latter case, they're usually called natural hybrids).

INDUMENTUM. The furry coating on the leaves of some rhododendrons. The color of indumentum can be an important decorative feature of the plant.

LEPIDOTE. Literally, scaly. The term is applied not only to a large number of rhododendron species but also to their hybrids, and refers to scales on the leaves or sometimes on the stems, buds, and flowers. The scales may not be obvious, but they are observable with a hand lens. Lepidote rhododendrons are generally smaller than standard large-leafed rhododendrons, and have the smaller leaves and profusion of smaller flowers characteristic of azaleas. (Other, smooth-leafed plants are known as elepidotes.)

SERIES. A group of closely related species within a genus (see page 8).

SPECIES. As used here, the word refers to a rhododendron that once grew somewhere as a wild plant and has since been propagated in cultivation either by seed, cuttings, grafting, or tissue culture. The species name is a lowercase word in italics follow-

TOP: 'Scarlet Wonder'
BOTTOM: 'Snow Lady'

ing the genus (for example, *Rhododendron catawbiense* is a species of rhododendron).

TRUSS. The flower cluster of a rhododendron.

VARIETY. As used here, the word denotes a single plant and all its progeny reproduced by cutting, grafting, or tissue culture. This single plant may be a hybrid or a selected individual from a species. The term *cultivar* is synonymous. If you buy a variety, you can be assured of getting a plant with a certain hue, marking, or form. Names of varieties or cultivars are designated by enclosure within single quotation marks ('Scintillation'), although the quotation marks have been eliminated for readability in the following entries. There is also a botanical variety (sometimes called *varietas*), which refers to a population within a species that differs in some respect from the basic species. These differences may include color, size, leaf characteristics, and, most notably, geographic distribution. In this case, variety is indicated by the third name in italics *(Rhododendron brachycarpum tigerstedtii)*.

TOP: 'Anah Kruschke'
BOTTOM: *Rhododendron augustinii* 'Electra'

TOP: 'Anna H. Hall'
BOTTOM: 'Autumn Gold'

A. BEDFORD

Vigorous, upright grower with large, dark, glossy green leaves and trusses of 3-inch pale to lavender blue flowers with distinctive dark blotches. Good plant for background planting or screening. 6'. −5°F/−21°C. ML. 4/3/5.

ALICE

Large plant, easy to grow, and tolerant of sun. Flowers are pink, in large, erect trusses. Received the British Award of Merit in 1910. 6'. −5°F/−21°C. M. 4/3−4/4−5.

ALOHA

Dense, well-rounded shrub with wrinkled, deep green leaves covered with white indumentum when young. Red buds open to deep pink flowers that develop paler purplish pink color for a two-tone effect. 3'. −15°F/−26°C. M. 3−4/4−5/4.

ANAH KRUSCHKE

Compact growth with dense, dark green foliage and trusses of lavender blue to reddish purple trusses. Exceptionally tolerant of heat and sun. A favorite in the Southeast and the warmer parts of California, although it can be sensitive to root rot in warm, wet soils. 6'. −15°F/−26°C. ML−L. 3−4/4/5.

ANNA H. HALL

Low, compact plant producing trusses of up to 15 flowers, pink in the bud and opening white. Leaves have brown indumentum. Slow growing. Exceptionally hardy. Can grow in hot summer climates if given shade. 3'. −25°F/−32°C. M. 3/3/4.

ANNA ROSE WHITNEY

Large, upright, shapely plant of great vigor with big leaves and 4-inch rose pink flowers in large trusses. Has done well in the Southeast and is a Northwest favorite. 6'. −5°F/−21°C. ML. 4/3/5.

R. AUGUSTINII

Species from western China and Tibet. Growth is compact and erect, with narrow, dark green leaves and 2-inch bell-shaped flowers in trusses of up to 6 flowers. Colors range from white to lavender pink to blue. Likes sun. Named superior blue selections include 'Barto Blue', 'Electra', 'Lackamas Blue', and 'Towercourt'. Hardiness rating may be too generous. 6'. −5°F/−21°C. EM. 4/3/3 − 4. Lepidote.

AUTUMN GOLD

Large plant with dark green foliage and pinkish orange flowers with deep orange blotch. Tolerates heat and performs better than other orange varieties in difficult situations. Has succeeded in the Southeast. 5'. −5°F/−21°C. ML. 3−4/3−4/4.

AZURRO

Dense, compact plant with attractive dark green, glossy foliage. Flowers are deep purple with a deeper purple blotch. Trusses 5 inches long hold as many as 14 flowers. 4'. −15°F/−26°C. L. 3−4/3−4/3−4.

BAMBINO

Compact plant with dark green foliage and trusses of flowers that mingle peach and yellow with a spotting of red. Large, colored calyx gives the effect of doubleness. 3'. −5°F/−21°C. M. 4/4/4.

BELLE HELLER

Hardy, sun-tolerant shrub with attractive foliage and large, ball-shaped trusses of white flowers with a showy gold blotch. 5'. −10°F/−23°C. M. 4/4/3.

BESSE HOWELLS

Broad, compact plant that produces many trusses of frilly, deep rose red flowers. 3'. −15°F/−26°C. EM. 3−4/3−4/3.

BIKINI ISLAND (BIKINI)

Hardy, open grower with smooth, flat foliage and large, bright scarlet flowers. One of the few very hardy pure reds. 5'. −20°F/−29°C. ML. Unrated.

BLUE DIAMOND

Bushy, erect plant with small leaves and a multitude of small blue flowers all along the stems. 3'. −5°F/−21°C. EM. 4/4/4. Lepidote.

BLUE ENSIGN

Hardy, sun-tolerant plant with lilac blue flowers blotched dark purple.

Resembles 'Blue Peter' but more compact. 4'. −15°F/−26°C. M. 4/3/4.

BLUE JAY

Strong-growing plant with bright green foliage. Lavender blue flowers have a pronounced reddish brown blotch. 5'. −10°F/−23°C. ML–L. 3/4/5.

BLUE PETER

Shiny green leaves and frilly lavender blue flowers with a deep purple blotch. Very heat tolerant; also tolerates cold and sun. Thrives in the eastern states. 4'−5'. −20°F/−29°C. M. 4/2−3/3.

BOULE DE NEIGE (SNOWBALL)

Medium-size, compact plant with an abundance of rounded trusses that look like snowballs. Very hardy to cold, and tolerates heat and sun. 5'. −25°F/−32°C. M. 3/3/3.

BOW BELLS

Mound-shaped plant that won't exceed 3 feet for many years. Cup-shaped pink flowers open from deeper pink buds in loose trusses of up to 7. Leaves are roundish and deep green, bronze on first emerging. Appreciates shade and dislikes excess fertilizing. 3'. −5°F/−21°C. EM. 3/4/3.

R. BRACHYCARPUM

Native to Japan and Korea. Leaves on mature plants have pale tan indumentum. Flowers are white, flushed pink and spotted green. The Korean variety *R. b. tigerstedtii* may well be the hardiest rhododendron, having withstood −45°F/−43°C. This plant also tolerates summer heat. 3'. −10°F/−23°C. VL. 3/3−4/2−3.

BURMA

Broad plant with dark green, wavy-edged leaves. Cardinal red flowers

TOP: 'Belle Heller'
BOTTOM: 'Boule de Neige'

TOP: 'Blue Peter'
BOTTOM: 'Bow Bells'

with heavy black spotting form erect conical trusses. A favorite red for the Northeast. 5'. −20°F/−29°C. ML. 4/3/3.

CALSAP

Exceptionally hardy, broad, densely foliaged plant with lavender buds that open to tall conical trusses of white flowers with a deep reddish purple blotch. Resembles 'Sappho' but hardier and with better plant form. 4'. −25°F/−32°C. ML. 4/3/4.

CAPISTRANO

Mounding growth, broader than tall. Dark green, somewhat roundish foliage. Flowers are clear light yellow, frilly, in well-rounded trusses. Some believe it may be the best hardy yellow rhododendron. 4'−5'. −15°F/−26°C. M. Unrated.

CAPTAIN JACK

Large leaves with slightly rolled edges. Trusses of blood red flowers have an unusual waxy gloss. 6'. 5°F/−15°C. ML. 4/3/4.

CAROLINE

Large plant with light green, slightly twisted leaves. Large flower trusses of orchid pink are fragrant, espe-

cially in warm weather. Resistant to root rot. 6'. −20°F/−29°C. ML. 3/4/4.

CARY ANN

Broad plant densely covered with dark green foliage. Prolific producer of trusses of flaring coral flowers. 3'. −5°F/−21°C. M. 3/4/4.

CASANOVA

Shapely, attractive plant with glossy foliage and pink buds that open to pale yellow with a strong orange blotch. A favorite plant for the Northeast. 4'. −25°F/−32°C. M. 4/5/4.

'Calsap'

'Casanova'

CATALGLA

A selected form of *R. catawbiense* 'Album'. Pink buds open to white flowers in large trusses. A notable parent for hybridizing hardy plants. 6′. −25°F/−32°C. ML. 3/3/4.

CATALODE See 'County of York'.

R. CATAWBIENSE. Catawba rhododendron

The native rhododendron of the southern Appalachian mountains and one prominent ancestor of many hardy rhododendrons. Plants variable in habit from dense to open. Flower color ranges from pinkish purple to deeper purple, rose, pink, and white. Thousands of these plants were once ripped from their native forests to furnish home gardens or large estates. Does not thrive in hot climates. 6′. −25°F/−32°C. ML−L. 3/3/4.

CATAWBIENSE ALBUM

Dark green foliage with somewhat convex leaves. White flowers with faint yellowish green spotting open from pink-tinged buds. Tolerates summer heat. 6′. −25°F/−32°C. ML−L. 3/3/4−5.

CATAWBIENSE BOURSAULT

Similar to *R. catawbiense* 'Album' but with pinkish lavender flowers. Exceptionally tolerant of cold and heat. 6′. −20°F/−29°C. ML−L. 2/3/4−5.

CHAMPAGNE See 'Dexter's Champagne', page 41.

CHEER

Vigorous plant producing a mound of glossy green foliage. Flower trusses are pink. 5′. −10°F/−23°C. EM. 3/3−4/4.

CHIONOIDES

Dense-growing, compact, rounded plant. Flower trusses are pure white with light yellow spotting. Endures sun and cold. 4′. −15°F/−26°C. ML. 3/4/4.

CHRISTMAS CHEER

Shapely plant with dark green foliage and extremely early trusses of light to deep pink flowers. Blossom color is variable from year to year; some years flowers are nearly white. Blooms at Christmas (or earlier) only where winters are mild, as in San Francisco. In colder regions, look for it in March. 4′. −10°F/−23°C. VE−E. 3/4/4.

CINNAMON BEAR

A compact *R. yakushimanum* hybrid with white, pink-tinged flowers. New growth is furry white, and older leaves have a heavy cinnamon brown indumentum. Beautiful in or out of flower. 3′. −15°F/−26°C. M. 3−4/5/4.

CONSOLINI'S WINDMILL

Deep green foliage and striking bicolored flowers—purplish red, with a white streak on each segment and a yellow flare on the uppermost segment. Tolerates both cold and heat. 5′. −15°F/−26°C. ML. Unrated.

COTTON CANDY

Big plant with trusses of large, pastel pink flowers so tall that they sometimes nod at the tips. 6′. 0°F/−18°C. M. 4/4/4.

COUNTY OF YORK (CATALODE)

Large plant with large white flowers of heavy substance in upright trusses.

TOP: *R. catawbiense* 'Album'
BOTTOM: 'Christmas Cheer'

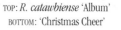

TOP: *R. catawbiense* 'Boursault'
BOTTOM: 'Crest'

Tolerates sun and cold. Resistant to root rot. 6'. −15°F/−26°C. M. 3−4/3/4−5.

CRATER'S EDGE

Dense, shrubby deciduous plant, bare in winter but covered with large flower buds that open into wide, flat, dark rose flowers. Useful for rock gardens and as bonsai. Considered best in dry climates, such as that of Colorado. 1½'. −15°F/−26°C. E. Unrated.

CREAM CREST

Compact and sun-tolerant plant with attractive foliage and a profusion of creamy yellow flowers. 3'. 0°F/−18°C. EM. 3/3−4/3−4.

CREST

Tall, open growth, tending to go bare toward the base. Large trusses of bright yellow flowers are considered the standard toward which yellow rhododendron flowers should aim. 6'. −5°F/−21°C. M. 4−5/3/3.

CRETE

Low, broad plant with white indumentum on new growth, beige indumentum on mature leaves. Buds are purplish pink, opening into tight, dome-shaped trusses of light purple flowers that fade to white. 4'. −25°F/−32°C. EM. 4/4−5/4.

CUNNINGHAM'S WHITE

Compact plant with white flowers marked with a yellow blotch opening from pink-tinged buds. Less fussy about soil than most rhododendrons, and may be considerably hardier to cold than its rating; a plant in Finland survived at −45°F/−43°C. Heat tolerant. 4'. −15°F/−26°C. ML. 2/3/4.

CYNTHIA

Large plant good for background or screening. Lavish producer of tall,

TOP: 'Cunningham's White'
BOTTOM: 'Daphnoides'

TOP: 'Cynthia'
BOTTOM: 'Edith Bosley'

rosy red trusses. A favorite in the Southeast, but not a success in the lower Midwest. 6'. −15°F/−26°C. M. 4/3/4.

DAPHNOIDES

Grown less for its small purple trusses than for its densely set, rolled, twisted, shiny green leaves. Late flowers help prolong the rhododendron season. 4'. −15°F/−26°C. ML. 2−3/4/4.

DEXTER'S CHAMPAGNE

Glossy bronze green foliage and white flowers suffused with cream, buff, pink, and apricot. 4'. −15°F/−26°C. M. 4/3/3.

DEXTER'S SPICE

Large plant producing loose clusters of very large (to 5 inches), very fragrant white flowers with faint green spotting. A score or more Dexter hybrids are being grown, with colors ranging from white through pink and lavender to red. Dexter didn't keep records of his crosses, but most plants are thought to contain

R. fortunei ancestry. They are sometimes called *Fortunei* hybrids. All are choice plants where winter temperatures are not extreme. 6'. −5°F/−21°C. L. Unrated.

EDITH BOSLEY

Like 'Purple Splendour' but much hardier. Compact, erect plant, well clothed with dark green leaves. Dome-shaped flower trusses are deep purple with a deeper purple eye. Tolerates heat, but subject to root rot in hot climates. 4'. −25°F/−32°C. M. 4/3/3−4.

ELISABETH HOBBIE

Low-growing plant with deep green leathery foliage and loose trusses of as many as 9 bright red, bell-shaped flowers. 2½'. −5°F/−21°C. EM. 4/4−5/3.

ELIZABETH

One of the most popular low-growing red rhododendrons; very widely planted in the Northwest and California. Attractive foliage sets off large flowers. The variety 'Elizabeth

TOP: 'Elizabeth'
BOTTOM: 'Etta Burrows'

TOP: 'English Roseum'
BOTTOM: 'Fatuosum Flore Pleno'

Red Foliage' is similar; its new foliage emerges red and keeps a red suffusion throughout the summer, darkening in winter. 3'. 0°F/−18°C. EM. 3−4/4/5.

ELSE FRYE

Small, deep glossy green leaves on a compact but somewhat open plant with attractive cinnamon bark. Flowers are white touched with pink, yellow in the throat, and intensely fragrant. Resembles 'Fragrantissimum', but more compact. 4'. 15°F/ −9°C. EM. 5/3/4.

ENGLISH ROSEUM (ROSEUM PINK)

Large plant with slightly rolled leaf edges. Flowers are lavender-toned pink. Plant is tough and undemanding. 6'. −25°F/−32°C. ML. 2−3/3/3−4.

ETTA BURROWS

Narrow, bristly, furry, deep green leaves and brilliant blood red flowers. 5'−6'. 5°F/−15°C. E. 4/4/3−4.

EVENING GLOW

Compact plant with narrow green leaves and a late show of deep yellow flowers. One of the more heat-tolerant yellows. 5'. −5°F/−21°C. L. 4/3/4.

FABIA G

This name is applied to a group of plants of identical parentage and similar appearance. Almost all have orange flowers. The choice 'Fabia Tangerine' is most readily available.

FABIA TANGERINE

Compact plant with reddish brown indumentum on the leaves. Flowers are brilliant orange, bell-shaped, in an open truss. 3'. 5°F/−15°C. M. 3/4/3−4.

R. FASTIGIATUM

Low, mounding plant with leaves ½ inch long or less. Flowers are lavender to purple, ½ inch broad, and cover the plant. A favorite rock garden shrub in the Northwest and Northeast. 1½'. −15°F/−26°C. M. 4/4/3−4. Lepidote.

FASTUOSUM FLORE PLENO

Open growth and rounded habit, with dark green leaves and trusses of lavender blue double flowers marked with a gold blotch. Flower center is filled with small lavender petaloids (petal-like structures). Highly tolerant of heat and sun. Subject to bud blast in hot, dry weather. 6'. −15°F/−26°C. ML. 3/3/3.

FIREMAN JEFF

Compact plant with medium green leaves. Trusses are brilliant pure red. Each flower has a large, red calyx that gives the effect of doubleness. 3'. 0°F/−18°C. M. 4/4/4.

R. FORTUNEI

Eastern Chinese species notable in its own right and a distinguished parent of hardy hybrids. Plant is erect, with large (to 8 inches) leaves and trusses of large (4-inch), sweetly fragrant flowers that open pink and fade to white. Hardy and easy to grow. Grows well in the hot, dry climates of Missouri, Arkansas, and Oklahoma. 6'. −15°F/−26°C. M. 4/4/4−5.

FRAGRANTISSIMUM

Stems are leggy and sprawling but can be trained on a trellis to 6 feet or more. Leaves are small to medium in size; the flowers are 4 inches, white tinged pink, and powerfully fragrant. 3'. 15°F/−9°C. EM. 4/2−3/4.

FULL MOON

Resembles 'Crest' but more compact. 4'. −5°F/−21°C. M. 4−5/ 4/2−3.

FURNIVALL'S DAUGHTER

Shapely, vigorous plant with heavily veined leaves and tall trusses of bright pink flowers blotched cherry red. 5'. −10°F/−23°C. M. 4−5/4/4.

GIGI

Large plant with medium-size leaves. Rose red flowers 3¼ inches wide are marked with deeper red spots. Trusses hold up to 18 flowers. 5'. −5°F/−21°C. ML. 3/4/(unrated).

GINNY GEE

One of the most highly rated dwarf rhododendrons. Dense, mounding plant with small, dark green leaves covered with an incredible profusion of inch-wide pink bells dotted white inside and out. Received a Superior Plant Award from the American Rhododendron Society. 2'. −10°F/−23°C. EM. 5/5/4. Lepidote.

GOLDEN GALA

Moderate-size, very hardy plant with pale yellow flowers that have faint green spotting in the upper lobe. Named in honor of the 50th anniversary of Ohio's Holden Arboretum. 3'. −20°F/−29°C. ML. 4/4/3.

GOLDEN TORCH

Deep green foliage with light brown indumentum beneath. Pink buds open to soft yellow flowers. 4'. 5°F/−15°C. ML. 4/4/4.

GOLDFLIMMER

Bright green foliage with light yellow variegation. Small trusses of ruffled lavender flowers appear late. 5'. −10°F/−23°C. L. 3/4−5/4.

GOLDFORT

Yellowish green leaves decked with light yellow flowers. Tolerates considerable cold and heat. One of the favored yellows in the Southeast. 5'. −15°F/−26°C. M. 3−4/3/4.

GOLDSWORTH ORANGE

Matte green leaves with red leaf stalks. Bright orange flowers appear in early summer. 5'. −5°F/−21°C. L. 3−4/3−4/3.

GOLFER

Nearly white "fur" on foliage almost throughout the growing season.

'Full Moon'

Undersides of leaves have pale gray indumentum. Flowers are pink, in tight clusters of up to 13. 1½'. −15°F/−26°C. EM. 3−4/5/4.

GOMER WATERER

Large plant well furnished with dark green leaves. White flowers open from pink buds and have a blotch of yellowish green. Tolerates both cold and sun; endures heat and drought better than most. 5'. −15°F/−26°C. ML. 3/4−5/4−5.

GRACE SEABROOK

Rich green foliage with light fawn indumentum on the underside of the leaves. Flowers are brilliant blood red. Valuable in the landscape as an early bright red. 6'. −5°F/−21°C. E−EM. 4−5/4/4.

GRAF ZEPPELIN

Big plant with dark, glossy foliage and compact trusses of up to 10 bright pink flowers with deeper pink edges. 5'. −15°F/−26°C. ML. 3/4−5/4−5.

GREER'S CREAM DELIGHT

Vigorous, bushy plant with large, smooth green leaves. Large trusses of cream flowers are notable for heavy substance and heat tolerance. 5'. −10°F/−23°C. ML. 4/4/4.

TOP: 'Fireman Jeff'
BOTTOM: 'Ginny Gee'

TOP: 'Fragrantissimum'
BOTTOM: 'Gomer Waterer'

FROM TOP TO BOTTOM: 'Halleluja!',
'Hardijzer's Beauty', 'Grace Seabrook',
'Halfdan Lem', 'Helene Schiffner'

HALFDAN LEM

Large plant with heavy stems, large leaves, and big tight, bright red trusses. Flowers have won awards. Plant may be hardier than listed rating. 5'. −5°F/−21°C. M. 4−5/4/4−5.

HALLELUJA!

Exceptionally heavy substance in stem, foliage, and flower. The trusses are large, the flowers bright rose red. 4'. −15°F/−26°C. M. 4−5/5/4−5.

HARDIJZER'S BEAUTY

An azaleodendron, a hybrid between a dwarf rhododendron and a Kurume azalea. Evergreen foliage turns red in winter. Pink blooms form all along the stems. Heat and sun tolerant. 3'. −5°F/−21°C. EM. 4/3−4/4.

HEART'S DELIGHT

Shapely plant with a dense covering of dark green leaves. Large trusses are a light, bright red with deeper markings. 5'. −10°F/−23°C. ML. 4/4/4.

HELEN DRUECKER

Long, wide, dark green leaves. Pink flowers to 4½ inches wide are held in trusses of up to 16. 5'. 5°F/−15°C. M. 4/3/3.

HELENE SCHIFFNER

Heavily foliaged plant of dark gray green. Pure white flowers with the lightest sprinkling of tiny dark dots form large, dome-shaped clusters. 4'. −5°F/−21°C. M. 4/4/3−4.

HELSINKI UNIVERSITY

Upright plant, taller than broad, with glossy green foliage and bright pink flowers with orange flecks. A hybrid of *R. brachycarpum* produced at the University of Helsinki in Finland, and extremely hardy to cold. 5'−6'. −38°F/−39°C. ML. Unrated.

HENRY'S RED

Extremely hardy plant, broader than tall, with trusses of 12 or 15 very dark red flowers. Highly rated in the Northeast. 5'. −25°F/−32°C. M. 3/3−4/4.

HOLDEN

Extremely hardy, compact plant with trusses of rose red flowers marked with a deeper blotch. Doing well in lower Midwest. 4'. −15°F/−26°C. EM−M. 3/3−4/4.

HONG KONG

Compact plant with shiny leaves and trusses of light yellow flowers. One of the hardiest yellows, and one of the few yellows highly rated in the Northeast. 5'. −20°F/−29°C. ML. 3/3/3.

THE HON. JEAN MARIE DE MONTAGUE (JEAN MARIE)

One of the favorite reds in the Northwest and California, and a good performer in the Southeast. Leaves are deep, rich green, the flower trusses bright red. Blooms at a young age. 5'. −5°F/−21°C. M. 4/4/4.

HORIZON MONARCH

Large, spreading plant with deep green leaves and red buds that open into huge trusses of pale greenish yellow flowers with a small red flare. Trusses can hold 15 flowers. 6'. 10°F/−12°C. M. 4−5/4/4.

HOTEI

Compact plant with medium-size leaves. Flowers 2½ inches wide are bright yellow and carried in tight, round trusses. One of the best yellows, but subject to root rot; needs excellent drainage. 3'. 0°F/−18°C. M. 5/4/3.

HURRICANE

Fast-growing yet compact plant with pink flowers marked with deeper pink. Offspring of 'Anna Rose Whitney' and 'Mrs. Furnivall'. 5'. 5°F/−15°C. M. 3−4/4/3−4.

R. HYPERYTHRUM

Upright growth habit, with long, narrow, wavy-edged leaves and 2-inch, funnel-shaped white flowers sometimes spotted red. Trusses hold 10 or more flowers. Native to Taiwan. Unusually tolerant of moist heat and is being used as a parent for plants that will grow in the Gulf Coast region. 3'. −15°F/−26°C. EM. 3/4/3−4.

ICE CUBE

Hardy plant with olive-tinged green leaves and cone-shaped trusses of creamy white flowers that have some lemon yellow in the throat. 4'−5'. −20°F/−29°C. ML. 4/3/4.

R. IMPEDITUM

Dwarf plant with tiny (½-inch) leaves of light grayish green. Flowers occur singly or in pairs and are ⅔ inch long. Color ranges from lavender blue to purple blue and can make a sheet of color. Plants set 15 inches apart can grow into a dense ground cover. 1'. −15°F/−26°C. EM. 4/4/3−4. Lepidote.

INGRID MEHLQUIST

Low, compact plant with deep green foliage; tan indumentum covers undersides of leaves. Pink buds open to trusses of pale pink fading to pure white. 3'. −20°F/−29°C. EM. 4/4/4.

JANET BLAIR

Large, attractive plant with trusses of frilly, light pink flowers that have a pronounced green flare. A good performer in the Southeast and lower Midwest. 5'. −15°F/−26°C. ML. 4/3/4.

JINGLE BELLS

Low-growing, densely foliaged shrub with bells that open bright red and pass through orange to yellow. 3'. 0°F/−18°C. M. 4/4/4.

JOE PATERNO

Mounding plant with shiny, dark green leaves and trusses of white flowers splashed with orange yellow. Good in hot climates. 5'. −20°F/−29°C. ML. 3−4/4/4.

JOHN COUTTS

Densely foliaged plant with long, pointed leaves and trusses of large salmon pink flowers. Late bloom helps prolong season. 4'. 0°F/−18°C. L. 4/3/4.

JOHNNY BENDER

Dense plant with glossy, heavy-textured deep green leaves. Flowers are also exceptionally heavy in texture, and deep bright red. 4'−5'. −5°F/−21°C. M. 3−4/5/4.

R. KEISKEI

Japanese species with 3-inch leaves and light to bright yellow flowers in clusters of 3 to 5. Two dwarf forms—one a foot tall, the other 6 inches—are hardier, and the latter is satisfactory in the Northeast. 'Yaku Fairy' is a selected form. All do well in the lower Midwest. 2'. −5°F/−21°C. EM. 4/3−4/4. Lepidote.

KEN JANECK. See
R. yakushimanum, page 53.

FROM TOP TO BOTTOM: 'The Hon. Jean Marie de Montague', *Rhododendron impeditum*, 'Hotei', 'Janet Blair', 'Joe Paterno'

TOP: 'Lem's Monarch'
BOTTOM: Loderi

TOP: 'Lavender Princess'
BOTTOM: 'Loder's White'

KIMBERLY

Compact plant with deep green foliage. Bright purple buds open to light pink, slightly fragrant flowers that blanket the shrub. 3'. −10°F/−23°C. EM. 3−4/4/4−5.

LAVENDER PRINCESS

Large but dense plant with dark green leaves. Large trusses are light lavender pink. Heat tolerant. 4'−5'. −20°F/−29°C. ML. 3/4/5.

LAVENDULA

Upright and compact shrub with small leaves and disproportionately large deep lavender flowers. 3'. −15°F/−26°C. M. 3−4/3−4/3−4. Lepidote.

LEE'S DARK PURPLE

Attractive dark green, wavy-edged leaves. Flowers are dark purple with a greenish flare. Thrives in the Southeast. 6'. −20°F/−29°C. ML. 2−3/3−4/4.

LEM'S CAMEO

Bronze foliage on emerging, dark green later on. Flower color is a blend of apricot orange, cream, and pink. The first rhododendron to win the seldom-offered Superior Plant Award. 4'. −5°F/−21°C. M. 5/3/3.

LEM'S MONARCH (PINK WALLOPER)

Big, heavy-branched plant with big leaves and huge, 12-inch trusses of bright pink. 6'. −5°F/−21°C. ML. 4−5/4 −5/4−5.

LEO

Dark green foliage; large trusses of extremely heavy, thick-textured, waxy, deep red flowers. 5'. −5°F/−21°C. ML−L. 5/3/3−4.

LITTLE GEM

Nearly prostrate growth, with shiny, dark green leaves and blood red flowers. 1½'. 0°F/−18°C. M. 4/4/3−4.

LODERI G

This group of hybrids includes some of the largest and most spectacular rhododendrons. All eventually become nearly treelike. Flowers are individually large, come in large clusters, and are extremely fragrant. The best known variety is 'Loderi King George', which has pale pink flowers that soon fade to white. 'Loderi Pink Diamond' is pastel pink, 'Loderi Venus' the deepest pink of the group. All the Loderis need lots of room and protection from strong sun and wind. They are best grown on large properties. 6'. 5°F/−15°C. M. 4/3−4/4.

LODER'S WHITE

Flower trusses are tall and cone-shaped, with white flowers that have a yellow throat and a faint pink picotee edge. Not one of the Loderi group mentioned above, and a more modest-size plant. 5'. 0°F/−18°C. M. 4/3−4/3−4.

LODESTAR

Plant has medium-large leaves. Flowers are 3½ inches across, white to extremely pale lilac, and come 15 to the truss. 5'. −20°F/−29°C. ML. 3−4/3−4/4.

LORI EICHELSER

A dense, compact plant twice as broad as tall, with deep green roundish leaves and good-sized deep reddish pink bells. 2'. −5°F/−21°C. EM. 4/4/4.

LUCKY STRIKE

Large, dull green leaves and 3-inch waxy, deep salmon pink flowers carried in conical trusses of 9. Plant does best in partial shade. 5'. 10°F/−12°C. ML. 3/3/4.

R. MACROPHYLLUM

Native species from Northern California to British Columbia. Individual flowers 2 inches wide are pinkish purple to white, spotted with reddish brown. Trusses may hold 20 flowers. The name, which means "large leaf," was conferred before Asiatic species with far larger leaves were discovered. A few named selections are occasionally seen. 6'. −5°F/−21°C. ML. 2−3/2−3/2.

MADRID

Flowers are bright pink with white stamens and a conspicuous red blotch. A relatively new introduction highly rated in the Northeast. 5'. −20°F/−29°C. ML. 3/3/3.

MANDA SUE

Compact plant with deep green leaves. Flowers are shell pink with a red picotee edge and a yellow throat. 3'. 0°F/−18°C. M. 4/3−4/3−4.

MANITOU (MANITAU)

Compact plant with small leaves and abundant flowers that open white and deepen to pink. Orange winter buds are a bonus. 3'. −25°F/−32°C. EM. 4/3/(unrated). Lepidote.

MARDI GRAS

Compact *R. yakushimanum* hybrid with large leaves and 3-inch unspotted blush white flowers in trusses of 12. 2½'. 0°F/−18°C. M. 4/4/4.

MARKEETA'S PRIZE

Large, sturdy plant with thick stems and large, deep green leaves. Exceptionally large trusses of bright red flowers. Heat tolerant. 5'. −5°F/−21°C. M. 5/4/4.

MARY BELLE

Medium-size leaves and clusters of 4-inch flowers that open salmon pink and fade to yellowish pink, spotted red. Favored in the Northeast. 5'. −15°F/−26°C. M. 3−4/3−4/4.

MARY FLEMING

Low, mounding plant with green foliage shading bronze in winter. Flowers are light yellow with lines of salmon pink. A favored selection for the Northeast. 3'. −15°F/−26°C. EM. 4/3/4.

MARYKE

Erect plant bearing matte green leaves on heavy stems. Flower trusses show a blend of pink and yellow. Heat tolerant. 5'. −5°F/−21°C. ML. 4/3/3.

MAXECAT

Exceptionally hardy hybrid between *R. maximum* and *R. catawbiense*. Large, fast growing, with dark green foliage and pink flowers. Heat tolerant. 6'. −25°F/−32°C. L. 4/3/4.

R. MAXIMUM. Rose Bay, Great Laurel

Native to much of the eastern United States and Canada. Large, fast-growing shrub or small tree with 10-inch leaves and small clusters of pink to white flowers that appear very late and are somewhat obscured by the leaves. Extremely hardy to cold. Name means "greatest"; it was conferred before much larger rhododendrons were discovered in Asia. 'Maximum Compactum' is a more compact plant. 'Maximum Roseum', a hybrid with *R. catawbiense*, has pink flowers. 5'. −25°F/−32°C. L−VL. 2/3/3−4.

MI AMOR

Striking plant for fanciers in mildest climates. Growth is open and lanky. Huge (6-inch) flowers are borne in clusters of 3 to 5. Flowers are powerfully fragrant, deeply bell-shaped, white with a yellow throat. 6'. 15°F/−9°C. M. 5/3/4.

FROM TOP TO BOTTOM: 'Madrid', 'Manitou', 'Maxecat', *Rhododendron maximum*, 'Mi Amor'

TOP: 'Mrs. Furnivall'
CENTER: 'Mrs. G. W. Leak'
BOTTOM: 'Naomi Nautilus'

MISSION BELLS

Sun-tolerant, compact plant with shiny, medium-size leaves and loose trusses of six to eight 2½-inch pale pink bell-shaped flowers. Slightly fragrant. 4'. −5°F/−21°C. EM−M. 3/4/3−4.

MIST MAIDEN. See
R. yakushimanum, page 53.

MOLLY ANN

Low, compact plant, with roundish leaves. Flowers rose pink, heavy in substance, and in upright trusses. 3'. −10°F/−23°C. EM. 4/4−5/5/4.

MOONSTONE

Low, compact mound with oval green leaves. Plant covers itself with creamy yellow flowers. 3'. −5°F/−21°C. EM. 3−4/4/3.

MRS. BETTY ROBERTSON

Moderate-size plant with rough-textured foliage. Flowers are light yellow, blotched red. 4'. −5°F/−21°C. M. 3/3/3.

MRS. CHARLES E. PEARSON

Old variety and a consistent award winner. The plant is erect and vigorous, with dark green leaves and trusses of light pink flowers with brown spotting. 6'. −5°F/−21°C. ML. 4/3−4/4.

MRS. FURNIVALL

Vigorous plant producing large, erect clusters of light pink flowers with a showy deep red blotch. Reportedly thriving in the eastern states. 4'. −15°F/−26°C. ML. 5/3−4/3−4.

MRS. G. W. LEAK

Large, vigorous plant with olive green foliage and light pink flowers with a reddish purple blotch. Older gardens may have this plant under the name 'Cottage Gardens Pride'. Good reports from Oklahoma, Missouri, and Arkansas. 6'. 0°F/−18°C. EM. 4/3/4.

MRS. T. H. LOWINSKY

Medium-size, compact plant with very dark green leaves. Tall trusses contain white flowers with a striking orange brown blotch. 5'. −15°F/−26°C. L. 4/3/4.

MYRTIFOLIUM

Low, dense grower with small leaves that are deep green in summer, bronze red in winter. Flowers are medium pink. Highly resistant to heat and sun. 3'. −15°F/−26°C. L. 3/5/4. Lepidote.

NANCY EVANS

Hybrid between the first-class parents 'Hotei' and 'Lem's Cameo'. Rounded plants flower freely. Orange red buds open amber and become golden yellow. Large calyx gives effect of doubleness. 3'. 5°F/−15°C. EM. 5/4/3−4.

NAOMI G

Many named hybrids exist within this group. All are large plants and heavy producers of fragrant flowers in the pink range, shading to yellow.

NAOMI NAUTILUS

Probably the best of the Naomis, rose pink flowers blended with orange, paling to yellow in the throat. 5'. −5°F/−21°C. M. 4/4/3.

NORMANDY

Broad, rounded plant with dark green leaves and bright pink flowers that have darker edges and an orange blotch. Popular variety in the Northeast. Fair performer in lower Midwest. 5'. −20°F/−29°C. ML. 4/4/4.

NORTHERN STARBURST

A tetraploid form of 'PJM Compact', possessing twice the gene count of

'Mrs. T. H. Lowinsky'

its parent, and producing larger deep purplish pink flowers with greater substance, stronger stems, and larger, thicker foliage that turns deep blackish purple in winter. 4'. −30°F/−34°C. E–EM. Unrated. Lepidote.

NOVA ZEMBLA

One of the most favored reds in the colder Northeast. Plant is sturdy and undemanding, with deep green leaves and trusses of dark red flowers with a darker red blotch. 5'. −25°F/−32°C. M. 3/3/4.

NOYO CHIEF

Attractive bright green, glossy, deeply veined leaves, coated beneath with fawn indumentum. Flower trusses are bright red. 5'. 10°F/−12°C. M. 4/4/3−4.

ODEE WRIGHT

Moderate-size, compact plant with shiny green foliage and large trusses of pure yellow flowers. 4'. −5°F/−21°C. EM. 4/4/3−4.

OLD COPPER

Attractive plant with orange flowers in late spring. Does well in the South—unusual for orange- and yellow-flowering rhododendrons. 5'. −5°F/−21°C. L. 4/3−4/4.

PAPRIKA SPICED

Compact plant with large yellow flowers that have a lavish sprinkling of paprika red spots beginning in the throat and nearly reaching the margin. Large yellow calyx. 3'. 0°F/−18°C. M. 5/3−4/3−4.

PARKER'S PINK

Large plant with large leaves and fragrant 3½-inch flowers of deep pink fading to white in the center and heavily spotted with red. Trusses hold 12 flowers. Good in lower Midwest. 5'. −25°F/−32°C. ML. 2/3/3.

TOP: 'Northern Starburst'
BOTTOM: 'Percy Wiseman'

TOP: 'Patty Bee'
BOTTOM: 'Pink Pearl'

PARTY PINK

Broad plant covered with wide, medium-size leaves. Trusses carry up to eighteen 3-inch flowers of purplish pink, paler toward the throat and spotted with yellow. Received a Superior Plant Award from the Great Lakes Chapter of the American Rhododendron Society. 5'. −20°F/−29°C. ML. 4−5/4−5/4−5.

PATTY BEE

Small plant well clothed with small (inch-wide) leaves that turn dark red in winter. Loose 6-flowered trusses of 2-inch lemon yellow flowers cover even young plants. Winner of a Superior Plant Award from the American Rhododendron Society. 1½'. −10°F/−23°C. EM. 5/4−5/4−5.

PERCY WISEMAN

Cross between *R. yakushimanum* and the orange-flowered Fabia. Compact plant has dark green foliage and peach yellow flowers that fade to white. An Oklahoma grower considers it his finest plant. 3'. −10°F/−23°C. M. 4/4/4.

PETER TIGERSTEDT

Upright, spreading plant with dark green leaves. Trusses of frilly white flowers have prominent violet flecks on upper segments. Bred at the University of Helsinki, and extremely hardy. For one parent, see *R. brachycarpum*. 6'. −33°F/−36°C. ML. Unrated.

PINK JEANS

Dark green foliage. Red buds open to purplish red flowers that shade toward yellowish white at the center, with red spotting and a red star in the throat. Rounded trusses contain 8 to 10 flowers. 4'. −5°F/−21°C. EM. 4/4/4.

PINK PEARL

Large plant with large, cone-shaped trusses of pale-throated pink flowers. Where hardy, this is the standard pink. 6'. −5°F/−21°C. M. 3/3/3.

PINK WALLOPER. See 'Lem's Monarch', page 46. Plants are identical or very similar.

TOP: 'PJM'
BOTTOM: 'Purple Splendour'

TOP: 'Point Defiance'
BOTTOM: 'Ramapo'

TOP: 'President Roosevelt'
BOTTOM: 'Sappho'

PJM

Dense, bushy, rounded plant with small broad leaves that turn purplish brown in winter. Flowering is exceptionally profuse, each terminal of the twiggy plant carrying a small truss of inch-wide purple pink flowers. Blooms with forsythia and daffodils. The New England favorite, and one of the hardiest of rhododendrons. Many people think it's an azalea because of its sheets of bloom. 'PJM Compact', 'PJM Elite', and 'PJM Regal' are similar. Survives winter cold and summer heat in Kansas and Oklahoma. 4'. −25°F/−32°C. E. 4/4/4. Lepidote.

POINT DEFIANCE

Very large plants with very large leaves and huge trusses of big white flowers with picotee pink edges. One of the Walloper group of exceptionally robust plants. 6'. −5°F/−21°C. EM. 5/4−5/4−5.

PRESIDENT LINCOLN

Tough, hardy plant producing tight trusses of light lilac pink flowers with a bronze blotch. 6'. −25°F/−32°C. ML. 2/3/3.

PRESIDENT ROOSEVELT

A plant for those who like variegation. Tall, cone-shaped trusses are red with white centers. Leaves are dark green with golden markings along and near the midrib. (Named for *Theodore* Roosevelt.) 4'. 0°F/−18°C. EM. 4/4/3.

PURPLE SPLENDOUR

Dense, dark green foliage and trusses of deep purple flowers with a nearly black blotch. Tolerates sun or shade. Needs excellent drainage. 5'. −5°F/−21°C. ML. 4/3/3.

RAINBOW

Erect plant with glossy foliage and tall trusses that sometimes nod toward the tips. Large flowers are white with a deep pink border. Strong two-tone effect. 6'. 0°F/−18°C. EM. 4/3/4.

RAMAPO

Low and compact in full sun, slightly taller in shade. New foliage is dusty blue, turning dark green. Heavy producer of pinkish violet flowers. Useful rock garden or low border plant. 2'. −25°F/−32°C. EM. 3/4/4. Lepidote.

RED EYE

Densely foliaged, vigorous, easy-to-grow plant. Flowers are deep reddish purple with an eye that starts out yellow and gradually becomes red. 5'. −10°F/−23°C. ML. 4/4/4.

RING OF FIRE

Compact plant with dense foliage. Flowers are yellow with a brilliant orange red rim. 4'. 0°F/−18°C. ML. 4/4/4.

ROCKET

Thick and heavily veined foliage, making a substantial-looking bush. Flowers are frilled, 2½ inches wide, pink with scarlet blotch. Truss is cone-shaped. 5'. −15°F/−26°C. M. 3/3−4/5.

ROSEUM ELEGANS

Olive green foliage and lilac pink flowers. Tolerant of heat and extreme cold. 6'. −25°F/−32°C. ML. 2/3/4.

ROSEUM PINK. See 'English Roseum', page 42.

ROYAL PURPLE

Shiny, deep green leaves and striking deep purple flowers. Blooms have a bright yellow eye. Tolerates both heat and cold. 4'–5'. –15°F/–26°C. ML. 3/3–4/4.

RUBY BOWMAN

🐾 Large plant with large, flat leaves. Long-lasting flower trusses are rose pink with deeper pink shading toward the center. 5'. –5°F/–21°C. M. 4/4/4.

RUBY HART

🐾 Dwarf plant with glossy, very dark green foliage and dark red flowers. 2'. 0°F/–18°C. EM. 4–5/4–5/4.

SAMOA

🐾 Wider than tall, with a dense clothing of rough, dark green foliage. Flowers are bright red in trusses of 15. 5'. –20°F/–29°C. EM. 4/4/3.

SAPPHIRE

🐾 Dense, dwarf grower with tiny, narrow leaves with edges rolled under. Flowers are small, profuse, light blue. Good in rock gardens, containers, as bonsai. 2½'. –5°F/–21°C. EM. 3/3/3–4. Lepidote.

SAPPHO

🐾 Open and rangy plant. Olive green leaves are medium, long, and narrow. Flowers are white with a conspicuous purplish black eye. Truss is round, compact. Good background plant. 6'. –15°F/–26°C. M. 3/2/4.

SAPPORO

🐾 Compact grower, slightly wider than tall, with attractive foliage. Flowers open pale lilac and age to pure white marked with a deep red purple blotch. Resembles a more compact 'Sappho'. 5'. –15°F/–26°C. ML. Unrated.

SCARLET ROMANCE

🐾 Broad plant, twice as wide as tall. Red flowers form large, round trusses. 4'. –25°F/–32°C. L. 3/3/3.

SCARLET WONDER

🐾 Low plant covered with shiny green leaves. Flowers are bright scarlet. Plant may be hardier than its rating; it has survived –45°F/–43°C in

'Scintillation'

Finland (perhaps protected by snow cover). 2'. –15°F/–26°C. M. 4/4/4.

SCINTILLATION

🐾 Heavy, waxy, deep green foliage. Pastel pink flowers have deep pink throat markings that age to brownish pink. An eastern favorite, and winner of a Superior Plant Award. One of the best in the lower Midwest. 5'. –15°F/–26°C. M. 4/4/4–5.

SEPTEMBER SONG

🐾 Compact plant, broader than tall, well covered by olive green foliage. Flowers are bright orange, shading to yellow in the center. 4'. 0°F/–18°C. M. 4–5/4/4.

COLD-TOLERANT RHODODENDRONS

If a rhododendron is cold-hardy, that generally means it has the ability to survive low temperatures and still bloom. It may be that the plant can survive the deep cold of midwinter, when it is fully dormant, or an early autumn frost before growth has fully ripened, or a late spring frost that might injure flowers or emerging growth buds. The so-called ironclads (plants listed as hardy to –25°F/–32°C or lower) can qualify on all these counts. What they cannot stand is strongly fluctuating winter temperatures accompanied by bright sunshine, strong winds, and capricious snow cover—conditions prevalent in most areas of the central United States. No rhododendron can survive those conditions without special attention.

Also look for hardy rhododendrons among those that have been bred in regions with severe winters. While these plants are less likely than the ironclads to survive under truly difficult conditions, they are more resistant to cold than the vast majority of hybrids developed in England, Holland, and the Northwest. Among such breeders are Dexter in Massachusetts, Hachmann

and Hobbie in Germany, Leach and Pride in western Pennsylvania and Ohio, Shammarello in northern Ohio, and Marjatta in Helsinki, Finland. Of their many introductions, the ones listed below will be found in the "Rhododendron Showcase."

DEXTER HYBRIDS Dexter's Champagne, Dexter's Spice, Gigi, Lavender Princess, Scintillation, Todmorden.

HACHMANN HYBRIDS Sapporo.

HOBBIE HYBRIDS Scarlet Wonder.

LEACH HYBRIDS Anna H. Hall, Bikini Island (Bikini), Burma, Capistrano, Crete, Golden Gala, Hong Kong, Janet Blair, Lodestar, Madrid, Normandy, Party Pink, Samoa, Sumatra, Summer Summit, Swansdown, Trinidad.

MARJATTA HYBRIDS Helsinki University, Peter Tigerstedt.

PRIDE HYBRIDS Joe Paterno.

SHAMMARELLO HYBRIDS Belle Heller, Besse Howells, Holden, Vernus.

TOP: 'Trinidad'
CENTER: 'Turkish Delight'
BOTTOM: 'Unique'

SHAMROCK

Compact, very low-growing, dense plant. Chartreuse flowers can appear as early as St. Patrick's Day. 1'. −5°F/−21°C. E. 3−4/4/4. Lepidote.

SHRIMP GIRL

Hybrid with *R. yakushimanum* as one parent. Plant is compact, with good dark green foliage and trusses of rose flowers. 3'. 0°F/−18°C. M. 3−4/3−4/3−4.

SKOOKUM

Slow-growing, low-mounding plant that branches freely. Leaves are dark matte green. Rounded trusses are bright red with prominent white stamens. 3'. −20°F/−29°C. ML. 4/4/4.

SNOW LADY

Low-growing plant with fuzzy, light green leaves and a big show of pure white flowers. 2½'. 0°F/−18°C. E. 3−4/4 −5/5. Lepidote.

SOLIDARITY

Fairly fast grower for a compact plant, with combined virtues of parents, 'The Hon. Jean Marie de Montague' and *R. yakushimanum*. Flower trusses open red, then turn pink, aging to nearly white. 3'. −15°F/−26°C. M. 4/4/(unrated).

SUMATRA

Low, broad plant with yellowish green foliage and bright scarlet flowers in a loose, open truss. 2'. −15°F/−26°C. EM. 4/4/3.

SUMMER SUMMIT

Very large plants with white flowers opening from pink buds. Flowers age to pure white with dark yellow spotting. Heat tolerant. 5'. −10°F/−23°C. VL. 3−4/3/4.

SUSAN

Large, fast-growing, shapely plant with shiny, dark green leaves and trusses of violet blue flowers. 6'. −5°F/−21°C. M. 4/4/−5/4.

SWANSDOWN

Strong-growing plant with medium large leaves. Flowers are 3 inches wide and white (rarely palest pink) with a strong constellation of yellow spots. Trusses are cone-shaped and may hold 20 flowers each. 5'. −20°F/−29°C. ML. 4/4/4.

TAURUS

Vigorous, shapely plant with deep green pointed leaves. Large round trusses are composed of large bright red bells with black spotting. Deep red winter buds are a bonus. Favorite in the Northwest and Southeast; reported thriving in Dallas. Superior Plant Award winner. 6'. −5°F/−21°C. EM. 4−5/4/4.

TIANA

Upright, open grower with dark green leaves. A hybrid between 'Sappho' and *R. yakushimanum*, resembling the former with its white flowers with deep burgundy butterfly-shaped blotches but a more compact plant. Heat tolerant. 4'. −5°F/−21°C. M. Unrated.

TODMORDEN

Strong grower with good foliage. Flowers are strikingly bicolored, rose with white throat and brownish spotting on the uppermost lobe. 5'. −15°F/−26°C. ML. 3−4/3/3−4.

TRINIDAD

Broad, free-flowering plant. Trusses contain up to 14 ivory yellow flowers with bright red rims. The hardiest of the two-tone yellow-red varieties. 4'. −20°F/−29°C. L. 4−5/4/4.

TRUDE WEBSTER

Highly rated variety and one of the first to win a Superior Plant Award. Leaves are large, wide, and slightly twisted, and the clear pink flower trusses are enormous. 5'. −10°F/−23°C. M. 5/4/4.

TURKISH DELIGHT

Medium-size, open-growing plant with large pink flowers. Popular in the Northeast. 4'. −20°F/−29°C. M. 3−4/3−4/3−4.

UNIQUE

Dense, mound-shaped plant with medium green leaves. Bright pink buds open to a creamy pale yellow. Flowers completely cover a well-grown plant. 4'. −5°F/−21°C. EM. 3/4−5/4.

VERNUS

🌸 Very hardy plant with dense foliage. Pale pink flowers are 2 inches across. One of the earliest large-flowering rhododendrons for the Northeast. 5'. −25°F/−32°C. EM. 3/3/4.

VIRGINIA RICHARDS

🌸 Compact, shapely plant with glossy, dark green foliage somewhat subject to mildew. Flowers open pink, then turn yellow with a dark red blotch. 4'. 0°F/−18°C. M. 4/4/4.

VULCAN

🌸 Large, shapely mound with flowers of bright red. Has succeeded in the Southeast. 'Vulcan's Flame' is very similar, perhaps a bit more compact in growth. Tolerates heat. 5'. −15°F/−26°C. ML. 4/4/4.

WESTON'S PINK DIAMOND

🌸 Upright plant, taller than broad, with small, yellow green leaves. Bright pink buds open to double pinkish purple flowers. 5'. −15°F/−26°C. E. 4/4/4. Lepidote.

WHITNEY'S ORANGE

🌸 Low-growing plant with leaves rolled at the edges and curled. Flower trusses are bright orange. 3'. 0°F/−18°C. ML. 4/3/4.

WILD AFFAIR

🌸 Fast-growing plant; needs some pinching when young to assure compact growth. Bright red flowers have golden yellow centers. 6'. −5°F/−21°C. ML. 4/3−4/4.

WINDBEAM

🌸 Very hardy shrub with small round leaves and apricot pink flowers fading to light pink. 4'. −25°F/−32°C. EM. 4/3/3−4. Lepidote.

WINSOME

🌸 Compact plant with small pointed leaves. Reddish flower buds make a winter show, then open into cherry red flowers. 3'. 0°F/−18°C. EM. 3−4/4/4.

WOJNAR'S PURPLE

🌸 Compact, spreading plant with a dense covering of dark green leaves. Flowers are reddish purple with darker edges and a darker blotch. 5'. −20°F/ −29°C. ML. Unrated.

R. YAKUSHIMANUM

🌸 Species native to Yakushima Island, Japan. Habit is low, tight, mounding.

🌸 New growth is covered with white felt. Older leaves are glossy dark green with brown indumentum underneath. Trusses contain up to ten 1½-inch flowers that open pink from deep pink buds, then fade to white. Proper name may be *R. degronianum yakushimanum*. One of the choicest rhododendrons, it is a parent of many hybrids that share its compact habit and attractive foliage. Tolerant of cold and surprisingly heat tolerant, passing both qualities to most of its hybrid offspring. 1'−4'. −25°F/−32°C. EM. 5/5/4.

Several named forms of the species exist: 'CHP' is tall, with pink buds opening to white. 'Ken Janeck' is somewhat taller and has deeper pink flowers. 'Koichiro Wada' is a low-growing, extremely dense plant. 'Mist Maiden' is taller than most. 'Yaku Angel' has narrow leaves and pure white flowers from pink buds. 'Yaku Picotee' has rose red flowers with white centers. Among the many popular hybrids are 'Yaku Prince', with pink flowers spotted reddish orange; 'Yaku Princess', with flowers of apple blossom pink and deeper accents; and 'Yaku Queen', with pink flowers shading paler inside and flared with yellow. The latter three are all 3-foot plants hardy to −10°F/−23°C, midseason to late bloomers, and rated 4/4/4 except for the last, which is rated 4/4/3.

TOP: 'Vernus'
BOTTOM: 'Wojnar's Purple'

TOP: 'Vulcan'
BOTTOM: *Rhododendron yakushimanum*

INTRODUCING CAMELLIAS

Camellias have long held a position of esteem in their native lands. In China, Japan, and Korea, the camellia motif is a familiar decoration that can be found on everything from architecture to textiles. The photographs in this section reveal not only the beauty of these flowers that enchanted the inhabitants of these areas, but also the great range of colors, sizes, floral forms, and styles. That such treasures should reach other parts of the world, there to be cultivated and enjoyed, was only a matter of time.

If you live in a coastal region, where camellias have traditionally been grown in North America, you are likely already aware of these splendid shrubs. If you're outside their generally recognized territory, take heart; new hybrids and breeding for cold tolerance are allowing gardeners to grow camellias in areas that once would have been considered too cold for them to survive (see "Camellia Country" on page 58).

The following pages explore the history and garden use of these beautiful plants. To find the plant that's right for your garden, look no further than the "Camellia Showcase" beginning on page 60.

A camellia bends under the weight of its April blooms.

WHAT IS A CAMELLIA?

Camellia japonica 'Alba Plena'

Grown as evergreen shrubs or small trees, camellias are noted for their medium to dark green, glossy leaves and abundance of blooms in fall and winter. They're versatile plants, blending into a garden border or serving as a centerpiece in a container. Camellias are often grouped with azaleas and rhododendrons because they enjoy the same growing conditions: well-drained soil rich in organic material; shelter from strong, hot sun and drying winds; and regular to moderate water. Given these conditions, they'll reward you with years of steady bloom.

CAMELLIAS IN THE WILD

Imagine yourself standing on a hillside in a semitropical forest where the lush vegetation is open rather than impenetrable. Surrounding you are a variety of handsome plants, some of which you recognize as wild rhododendrons and azaleas not yet ready to burst into bloom. Included in this forest undergrowth are specimens of one especially attractive shrub—neater than the others, with foliage that appears polished. At the moment, they are in full bloom—it seems with as many flowers as leaves. Some are bright red, some pink, others white, while still others show variegations of these colors. Closer inspection reveals that some of these shrubs are really 30-foot trees with trunks a foot thick. These plants are, of course, wild camellias.

Beneath your feet is a thick, soft carpet of decaying leaves and twigs. A wind comes up—brisk in the treetops but more moderate below—bringing rain. The shower is heavy, but the abundant moisture that reaches the forest floor is quickly absorbed by the natural mulch and the humus-rich, porous soil. Such showers are frequent but brief. The clouds depart, and the sun returns—filtered, of course, by the trees—leaving behind freshened air, washed leaves, and moist soil.

Such a scene can be found nearly anywhere in camellias' native range, a roughly S-shaped region that extends from the subtropical mountainous valleys in southwestern China and northern Indochina up the China coast, covering Taiwan and other islands, to its northernmost limits in Korea and Japan. Though it's a temperate zone, variations in the severity of the winter cold throughout the camellia range affect the hardiness of various species and hybrids. During the growing season, the whole territory receives generous rainfall.

Camellia reticulata 'Captain Rawes'

A HISTORY OF CAMELLIA CULTURE

Though precise dates are difficult to establish, it is certain that one species, *Camellia sinensis,* was grown extensively in China at least 2,000 years before Christ—not for the beauty of its flowers but for its leaves, which were used to make tea. A thousand years later, in eastern Asia, camellia blossoms were used as adornments at festive occasions and as symbols of particular virtues.

Camellia sinensis

Even the seeds were put to use, as a source of oil used in food preparation or as a hair dressing.

By A.D. 800, when Charlemagne had consolidated central Europe into what would be known for 1,000 years as the Holy Roman Empire, there were on record in China descriptions of 72 different forms of *C. reticulata*.

FROM ASIA TO THE WEST

How the first camellias reached Europe is no mystery: they came by ship. But precisely when and to what country is unclear. It is probable, though not documented, that the first *C. japonica* plants arrived in Portugal in the mid- to late 1500s. That they were introduced in England in the early 1700s is a matter of record. It is also certain that *C. japonica,* the most familiar camellia of gardens, was described and named by the Swedish botanist Linnaeus in 1735. The name *camellia* commemorates Georg Joseph Kamel (1661–1707), a Moravian Jesuit who worked in the Philippines as a pharmacist, physician, and botanist—and who probably never saw a camellia.

But for modern gardeners, the history of camellias really begins in 1792, when a ship of the British East India Company carried to England a camellia designated 'Alba Plena'. Even now, nearly 200 years after its introduction to the West, 'Alba Plena' remains one of the most popular and widely available *C. japonica* varieties. How old it actually is can only be conjectured.

'Alba Plena' was in the vanguard of the many old Chinese garden varieties of *C. japonica* that would be imported from China; a few others ('Donckelarii', for example) are still in the nursery trade. The first *C. reticulata,* 'Captain Rawes', reached England in 1820. When they were introduced to the European gardening public, the Chinese garden names of the camellias were changed (and often Latinized) to make them more euphonious to the European ear.

Soon after the earliest imports flowered, enterprising European nurseries started raising new varieties from seed. Italy may have led other countries in the production of new varieties during the 19th century, but many also came from France, Belgium, Germany, England, and Portugal. By the end of the century, hundreds of named varieties of *C. japonica* had been offered for sale.

THE OPENING OF JAPAN

Although Japan's horticultural history is less ancient than that of China, it is likely that *C. japonica* was being grown and selected as a garden ornament in Japan as far back as the 1400s. But during the 18th- and early 19th–century heyday of horticultural importing from the Far East, Japan was virtually closed to trade with European nations. Not until this commercial isolation was ended by treaty in 1859 were the riches of Japanese horticulture made available to amateur gardeners.

When introduced to the rest of the world, the Japanese *C. japonica* garden varieties of camellia also often left behind their

Camellia blooms add color to a winter garden.

lovely, sometimes centuries-old original names: Thus, 'Usu-Otome' became 'Pink Perfection' in California and was introduced in Germany as 'Frau Minna Seidel'. Similarly, the old favorite 'Herme' came to Germany originally as 'Hikaru-Genji'. Only a few 19th-century Japanese imports such as 'Daikagura' managed to retain their original and colorful names.

CAMELLIAS TODAY

In the eastern Asian homeland of the camellia, there are at least 80 different species. But only four are generally available in North American nurseries: *C. japonica, C. reticulata, C. sasanqua,* and *C. hiemalis*. Japonicas, reticulatas, and sasanquas are the camellia gardener's "big three" (hiemalis varieties are usually cataloged with the sasanquas).

In addition, various other species, some not spectacular in themselves, can offer the big three additional desirable characteristics through hybridization. Plant enthusiasts tend to be incorrigible dreamers, and among camellia enthusiasts, three dreams of long standing have been greater hardiness to cold, flower fragrance, and yellow color. Two of these have already been partly fulfilled, and the other now seems delectably possible.

Fragrance is already present in several of the less spectacular species, and some hybrids have been produced that combine fragrance with improved flowers. Persistent hybridizing should, in time, add distinct fragrance to the striking blossoms of japonicas and even reticulatas.

Hardiness to cold is also improving. The extra-hardy camellias (see page 68) are good choices if you live in a region considered too cold for standard camellias.

Finally, yellow-flowered camellia species are becoming available in the United States, on a limited basis, as discussed on page 68.

CAMELLIA COUNTRY

In North America, "Camellia Country"—where *Camellia japonica* and *C. sasanqua* will take a normal winter in stride—embraces the Atlantic and Gulf Coasts of the United States and the Pacific Coast of the United States and Canada, extending northward and inland wherever winter temperatures remain above 0°F/–18°C.

But "Camellia Country" is expanding its borders, thanks to the breeders of cold-tolerant camellias and to extensive testing and reporting by camellia fanciers. The darker shaded portions of the map below show safe camellia growing territory . Note, however, that even here camellias should be sited carefully and given winter protection during unusually cold spells. Roots will be severely damaged at about 20°F/–7°C (hence the need for good winter mulch in colder regions), but many japonicas can survive 0°F/–18°C or even lower if sheltered from wind and sun, and if the temperature drop is gradual.

The lightly shaded areas have not been traditional camellia-growing regions, but the hardier kinds deserve a trial here. Some new camellias will withstand temperatures as low as –15°F/–26°C. Protection from winter sun and wind is essential, and there is always a chance that a killer cold wave could wipe out the plants. Still, camellias are worth the risk. Success in colder areas will depend on weather, the gardener's knowledge and skill, and the plant itself. Healthy, established plants grow in areas that in theory should be too cold for camellias to survive outdoors (around New York City, Long Island, and coastal Connecticut, for example).

Camellias can, of course, be grown in greenhouses. Indeed, the early centers of camellia culture in the United States were New York, Boston, and Philadelphia, and most of the camellias planted in the South came from greenhouses in the North.

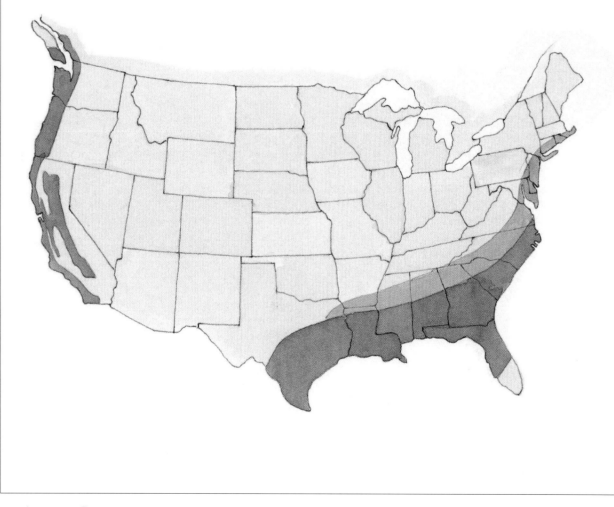

CAMELLIAS IN THE LANDSCAPE

A forest of camellias in a wooded garden.

Even if camellias never flowered, most would rank high on any list of recommended landscape shrubs. But as they are capable of sending forth beautiful blossoms during the months when garden color is at low ebb, camellias rise above the category of "recommended"—even approaching that of "essential" for some aficionados. Only climate limits their use, and as noted in "Gardening in Containers" (page 97) and "Winter Protection" (page 102), the effects of climate can be modified or circumvented by gardeners in less-than-favorable regions who are captivated by the camellia's charms.

The descriptions of principal species and hybrids on pages 60 through 69 reveal the diversity of flowers, flowering times, foliage, and plant habits at the gardener's disposal; a look at where they grow in the United States (see "Camellia Country" on the opposite page) will give you an overview of the conditions they prefer. With this information in mind, consider the various landscaping possibilities camellias offer.

WOODLAND GARDEN. The gardener lucky enough to have dappled shade from tall trees can use camellias as nature distributed them in the forests of eastern Asia. Casually grouped around meandering paths under high shade according to color, size, type, and bloom season, camellias can help you achieve a fusion of natural beauty and artistic control.

BASIC SHRUBBERY. The idea may seem dull, but think of the need in every garden for basic shrubbery, and then reflect on the virtues of using camellias for such plantings. Whether along a fence or walkway, against house walls, or as a backdrop to lower shrubs, perennials, or annuals, camellias can give a landscape dignity and polish throughout the year, punctuated by colorful blossoms in their season.

ACCENT SPECIMEN. Visualize just one camellia plant in full flower; then imagine it placed in a partly shaded garden area that you'd like highlighted during the year's least colorful period. A camellia could greet you beside your

Espaliered camellias line the side of a house.

front door or welcome you at the garden entrance. A tubbed specimen might become the focal point of an intimate patio, while a large japonica or tall reticulata under high shade trees could be a garden beacon in a picture-window view.

Trained as espaliers, camellias can lend both foliage and floral beauty to walls and fences where shade or space restrictions rule out other—and less attractive—choices. Among the sasanquas are some of such pliable growth that you can consider them almost as vines.

CONTAINER PLANTS. Camellias take so well to container culture that many gardeners actually prefer growing specimens that way. When growing them in containers, you have greater control over water and nutrients, and you always have the option of moving plants to a more favorable or more conspicuous location.

HEDGES. Many sasanquas, many hybrids, and some japonicas are both vigorous and dense enough to be massed in a line as hedge and barrier plantings. They'll look their best when only lightly clipped—just enough to remove straggling growth—rather than formally sheared. When camellias are clipped this way, they'll also produce more blooms.

GROUND COVERS. The more willowy or vinelike sasanquas can easily be coaxed into service as ground cover plantings. All year they'll offer handsome, polished foliage, and in autumn they'll nearly smother themselves with blossoms.

CAMELLIA SHOWCASE

Camellia varieties number in the thousands. The listings that follow include popular and widely available sorts, grouped according to type: japonicas, reticulatas, sasanquas, and various hybrids. The correct names of plants, as well as descriptions of flower and plant forms, are in accordance with Camellia Nomenclature, *the official nomenclature guide of the American Camellia Society. Special terms and abbreviations are described below.*

SEASON OF BLOOM. Camellias can bloom from fall through spring. The season of bloom is very different for different species, and thus "early blooming" and "late blooming" must be correlated with the flowering season of the species. Also, "early" and "late" have different meanings relative to the climates in which camellias are grown. The following breakdown indicates the expected time of bloom in a mild climate, such as California, for the spring-blooming camellias, including *Camellia japonica.*

> E = Early   (October to January)
> M = Midseason   (January to March)
> L = Late   (March to May)

In colder areas, such as North Carolina, early varieties will begin to flower in October or November, but in many years flowering mostly stops in midwinter and begins again in late February or early March. The remainder of the flowering season follows rapidly and is mostly completed by late April.

For the sasanquas and other fall-blooming species, early, midseason, and late may be designated as follows:

> E = Early   (September and early October)
> M = Midseason   (October and early November)
> L = Late   (November to January or later)

In the listings, the letter abbreviation E, M, or L following the plant name indicates the season of bloom.

FLOWER SIZE. Notation of typical flower size (in diameter) is based on the following scale:

> Miniature   (1½ inches or less)
> Small   (1½ to 3 inches)
> Medium   (3 to 3½ inches)
> Medium large   (3½ to 4 inches)
> Large   (4 to 5 inches)
> Very large   (Over 5 inches)

'Elegans' (Chandler)

ALTERNATE NAMES. If a variety is sometimes sold under other names, these synonyms appear immediately following the description.

HARDINESS. Some varieties that have proved reliably cold-hardy to 0°F/−18°C are designated by the letter H at the end of the entry. Note, however, that flower buds may be damaged at this temperature. A list of extra-hardy camellias is provided with the hybrid camellia entries, on page 68. In colder areas, camellia plants, even extra-hardy ones, should be mulched and given protection from winter wind and sun.

A FEW SPECIAL TERMS

The words that follow have special meanings when applied to camellias.

FIMBRIATED. Fringed. It refers to petal edges that are fringed in the manner of carnations.

PETALOIDS. The small petal-like organs in the center of a camellia flower. They may be reduced petals or modified stamens.

RABBIT EARS. Fluted (folded) petals that stand upright in the center of a flower.

SPORT. A spontaneous mutation that results in a change of color or flower form (flower color sports are frequently unstable).

STAMENS. The yellow filaments—actually pollen-producing organs—that appear prominently in the center of many camellia flowers. The mass of stamens and pistils in a camellia flower is called a boss.

VARIEGATED. Spotted, marbled, flecked, striped, or otherwise marked with a second color. On red and pink camellia varieties, the variegation is usually white; variegated forms of white varieties are marked with pink or red. Markings may be inconsistent among individual flowers: some may be striped, some flecked, some stippled; some may be half one color, half the other—or others. Indeed, some of the flowers may be entirely of one color.

CAMELLIA JAPONICA

TOP: 'Berenice Boddy'
BOTTOM: 'Betty Sheffield Supreme'

Mention the word "camellia," and most people automatically think of *C. japonica*. Varieties of this species were the first to enter the European horticultural world, and they have dominated the camellia nursery trade ever since.

Within this species occur all the camellia flower forms, from the simple five-petaled single to the completely double, and flowers of a wide variety of colors: purest white, all shades of pink from blush to deepest rose, light to dark red, and variegations of these colors in differing patterns. Blossom sizes range from miniatures less than 2 inches across to lush 7-inch stunners.

These camellias generally have the best-looking foliage—rich, glossy green, and abundant. Ultimately, japonicas may reach heights of 30 feet with a spread nearly equal to that. But they may take more than one person's lifetime to achieve such proportions.

Partly because of its great number of varieties, this species also embraces the longest bloom season of all camellias, covering a period of about 6 months. The earliest varieties start to bloom in late autumn, and the latest finish in late spring. A careful selection of varieties can keep your garden in flower through the leanest floral period of the year.

A class of japonicas known as Higo have single flowers and a notably large boss of stamens. They are cherished here and in Japan as bonsai subjects, and also valued in this country as landscape plants because of their profusion of simple, natural-looking blossoms. Flowers of the Higos have the additional merit of dropping cleanly from the plant when finished blooming.

ADOLPHE AUDUSSON. M

Large, dark red, semidouble flowers with broad, wavy petals and a boss of gold stamens. Fast, upright grower with somewhat open growth. Prolific bloom. There is a variegated form. Synonyms: 'Adolphe', 'Audrey Hopfer'.

ALBA PLENA. E–M

Medium, pure white, formal double flowers with a short bloom period. Very old variety imported to Britain in 1792. Good container plant.

BERENICE BODDY. M

Medium, light pink, semidouble flowers showing deeper pink tone at the tip of each petal. Vigorous, erect plant. H.

BETTY SHEFFIELD. M

Medium to large, white, peony-form flowers marked with red and pink. Medium upright growth. The parent of numerous sports that resemble it except in color.

BETTY SHEFFIELD SUPREME. M

Like 'Betty Sheffield' but with a deep rose border to each petal. 'Betty's Beauty' has a narrower pink border. 'Betty Sheffield Coral' is a solid-color coral. 'Betty Sheffield Blush' is a sport with pale pink flowers and darker pink markings. (The color and color pattern of 'Betty Sheffield' sports are unstable, so new floral variants will be observed on these varieties from time to time.)

BLOOD OF CHINA. L

Medium to large, deep red, semi-double to loose peony form. Tall, broad, dense plant. Late bloom a disadvantage in hottest climates. There is a variegated form. H.

CAMELLIA FLOWER FORMS

Single

Semidouble

Formal Double

Peony form

Anemone form

Rose form

TOP: 'Bob Hope'
BOTTOM: 'C. M. Wilson'

TOP: 'Drama Girl'
BOTTOM: 'Elegans Supreme'

BOB HOPE. M–L

Large to very large, very dark red, irregular semidouble. Medium slow, upright, compact habit.

C. M. HOVEY. M–L

Medium to large, dark red, formal double flowers. Faded blooms shatter (petals fall individually instead of coming off as a unit). Fast, upright, somewhat open growth. Old variety with many synonyms; often sold as 'Colonel Firey' or 'William S. Hastie'.

C. M. WILSON. E–M

Large, light pink, anemone-form flower. A sport of 'Elegans (Chandler)', with the same medium, spreading growth. H.

CARTER'S SUNBURST. E–L

Large to very large, pale pink, semidouble to peony-form flowers marked with deeper pink streaks.

Spreading growth. 'Carter's Sunburst Blush' is pink striped deeper pink and bordered with white.

CHANDLERI ELEGANS. See 'Elegans (Chandler)', below.

CLARK HUBBS. M

Large, dark red flowers of full to loose peony form, with fimbriated petals. Upright, compact plant. 'Clark Hubbs Variegated' has white marbling.

CONRAD HILTON. E

Sport of 'Daikagura' with similar growth habit. Flowers are medium to large, pure white, peony in form.

COVINA. M

Small, rose red, semidouble to rose-form flower. Compact, sun-tolerant plant; profuse bloomer. Vigorous spreading habit. Good for hedges.

DAIKAGURA. E–L

Medium to large, peony-form flowers with many color variants ranging from bright rose red through white. Bloom starts very early and extends over a long season in California. Medium, compact growth.

DEBUTANTE. E–M

Medium to large, light pink flowers of full peony form. Upright and vigorous. A very heavy bloomer. Synonym: 'Sara C. Hastie'. H.

DONCKELARII. M

Medium to large, red, semidouble flowers that show a wide range of marbling in white. Plant is slow growing, bushy. Introduced from China in 1834. H.

DR. TINSLEY. M

Medium, pale pink, semidouble flowers. Petals shade to deeper pink at petal edges. Compact, upright plant. H.

DRAMA GIRL. M

Very large, salmon pink, semidouble flowers with broad, wavy petals. Plant is vigorous and open, with somewhat pendulous branches. There is a variegated form.

ELEANOR HAGOOD. L

Medium, pale pink, formal double flowers. Late flowers sometimes fail to open well. Vigorous, upright bush.

ELEGANS (Chandler). E–M

Variety dates from 1831. Flowers are large to very large, anemone in form, with rose pink guard petals and a central mass of rose pink petaloids sometimes spotted with white. Medium, spreading growth. If central leader is damaged, plant is slow to put on height. The source of numerous fine sports. Synonyms: 'Chandleri Elegans', 'Francine'. The variety 'Elegans (Chandler) Variegated' is similar but has white marbling. 'Elegans Supreme' has deeply fimbriated petals.

ELEGANS CHAMPAGNE. E–M

Resembles 'Elegans (Chandler)', but flowers have very deep petal serrations.

ELEGANS SPLENDOR. E–M

Has flower form and plant habit of the Elegans group, but flower is light pink edged with white. Petals are fimbriated.

FINLANDIA. E–M

Medium large, white, semidouble blooms with wavy, fluted petals. Free flowering. Medium, compact growth. 'Finlandia Variegated' is similar, but with light streaks of dark red at petal edges. H.

FIRCONE. M

Miniature, blood red, semidouble with petals regularly spaced like scales on a fir cone. Profuse bloom. 'Fircone Variegated' has white markings. Vigorous and bushy.

FLAME. M

Medium to large, deep red, semidouble flowers. Compact, upright, vigorous growth. There is a variegated form. H.

FRANCINE. See 'Elegans (Chandler)', above.

GIGANTEA. M

Very large, deep red flowers strongly marked with white; semidouble to anemone or peony form. Plant is vigorous, upright, and open. Synonyms: 'Emperor Wilhelm' and 'Magnolia King', among many others.

TOP: 'Finlandia'
BOTTOM: 'Gigantea'

TOP: 'Glen 40'
BOTTOM: 'Hawaii'

GLEN 40. M–L

Medium to large, deep red, formal double to rose-form flowers. Slow, compact, upright grower. Synonym: 'Coquetti'. H.

GRAND SLAM. M

Large to very large, dark glowing red, semidouble to anemone form. Vigorous, open growth. 'Grand Slam Variegated' has white markings. H.

GUILIO NUCCIO. M

Large to very large flowers of rich coral pink verging on red; semidouble in form. Fluted, erect "rabbit ear" petals give the flowers great depth; they resemble those of the reticulatas, and are equal in size. Upright, vigorous grower. Many consider this plant the finest japonica. 'Guilio Nuccio Variegated' is similar but with white marbling.

HAWAII. E–M

A sport of 'C. M. Wilson', one of the Elegans group, with the same medium, spreading habit. Flowers are medium to large, light pink, peony form with fimbriated petals.

HERME. M

Medium to large, pink, semidouble flowers with a white border and occasional stripes of deeper pink. Upright, slender plant. Synonym: 'Jordans Pride'. H.

HIGH HAT. E

Sport of 'Daikagura'. Medium to large, light pink, peony-form flowers. Medium-growing, compact plant. Long bloom season. H.

JOSHUA E. YOUTZ. E

Large, pure white, peony-form to formal double flowers. Seedling of, and similar to, 'Daikagura'.

TOP: 'Lady Clare'
CENTER: 'Magnoliaeflora'
BOTTOM: 'Mrs. D. W. Davis'

KONA. M–L

A sport of 'Hawaii', one of the Elegans clan. Medium to large flowers of unusual greenish white in a tight, full peony form with fimbriated petals.

KRAMER'S SUPREME. M

Large to very large, bright red flowers with orange undertone; peony form with petals and petaloids massed together. Vigorous, upright grower. Can take some sun. Many people can detect a slight fragrance.

KUMASAKA. M–L

Medium, rose pink flowers vary from peony form to rose form. Very heavy bloom on a rather narrow, dense-growing, vigorous plant. Good tolerance to sun and cold. 'Kumasaka Variegated' has white marbling. H.

LADY CLARE. E–M

Large, rose pink, semidouble flowers. Blooms drop cleanly when spent. Shrub is vigorous, fast growing, spreading, and arching. Leaves are dark green, glossy. H.

LADY KAY. M

Sport of 'Ville de Nantes'. Medium to large, deep red flowers marbled with white; loose to full peony form. Petals are fimbriated. Slow, compact growth. H.

LALLAROOK. M–L

Medium to large, rose pink, formal double flowers often marbled with white. Edges of petals curve backward. Medium, compact growth with laurel-like foliage. Synonyms: 'Laurel Leaf', 'L'Avenire'.

LOTUS. E–M

Very large, pure white, semidouble flowers with a prominent central boss of yellow stamens. Plant is vigorous and spreading, with light green foliage. Blooms last better if kept from cold, rain, strong sun.

MAGNOLIAEFLORA. M

Medium, blush pink, semidouble blossoms. Free-flowering plant of medium size, compact habit. H.

MARC ELEVEN. M–L

Large, bright red, semidouble flowers with "rabbit ear" petals like those of 'Guilio Nuccio' or many of the reticulatas. Central boss of yellow stamens is prominent. Fast, spreading growth.

MARGARET DAVIS. M

Medium, creamy white to white flowers streaked and edged with red; peony form. Slow, upright growth habit. 'Margaret Davis Picotee' is similar, but red petal borders are narrower.

MATHOTIANA. M–L

Very large, deep purple–toned red, formal double to peony flowers. Vigorous, compact, upright plant. Good hot-weather performer. Synonyms: 'Julia Drayton' and 'William S. Hastie', among many others. H.

MATHOTIANA SUPREME. M–L

Sport of 'Mathotiana', which it resembles except that flowers are semidouble, with petals and stamens interspersed.

MAUI. M

Sport of 'Kona', and hence of 'Elegans (Chandler)'. Large, white, anemone-form flowers with wavy guard petals. Habit resembles that of others in Elegans clan.

MRS. CHARLES COBB. E–M

Medium to large, deep red, peony-form to semidouble flowers with large, loosely arranged petals. Vigorous, bushy plant well adapted to hot weather.

MRS. D. W. DAVIS. M

Very large, blush pink, semidouble flowers. Strong, upright, somewhat open plant. 'Mrs. D. W. Davis Descanso' is similar, but with peony form. 'Mrs. D. W. Davis Special' is also similar, with rose form.

MRS. TINGLEY. M–L

Medium, silvery salmon pink, perfect formal double flowers. Blooms are freely produced on a medium, upright plant.

NUCCIO'S CAMEO. E–L

Medium to large, coral pink, formal double flowers; occasional flowers are rose form. Upright, compact, bushy plant; long bloom season.

NUCCIO'S GEM. E–M

Medium to large, white, formal double. Medium, bushy, upright grower.

NUCCIO'S JEWEL. M–L

Medium, white flowers, shading to coral pink at the edges; loose to full peony form. Medium, bushy grower.

NUCCIO'S PEARL. M–L

Medium, blush white, formal double with pointed petals; both center and outside petals are tinted deeper pink. Vigorous, upright habit.

NUCCIO'S PINK LACE. E–L

Medium large, blush pink, anemone- to peony-form flowers with a long bloom season. Medium, upright growth.

PINK PERFECTION. E–L

Small, light pink, formal double flowers. Plant is vigorous, dense, and upright. Produces many flowers over a long season despite considerable bud drop. Synonyms: 'Frau Minna Seidel', 'Usu Otome'. H.

POPE PIUS IX. See 'Prince Eugene Napoleon', below.

PRINCE EUGENE NAPOLEON. M

Medium to large, rosy red, formal double flowers, with neatly shingled petals that grow smaller toward center of flower. Strong, compact plant. Upright habit. Synonym: 'Pope Pius IX'.

PROFESSOR CHARLES S. SARGENT. M

Medium, dark red, peony-form blossoms tightly packed with petals. Tough, easy-to-grow plant; compact, upright. H.

PURITY. M–L

Medium, pure white, rose-form to formal double flowers. Plant is strong, upright. H.

R. L. WHEELER. E–M

Very large, rose red, semidouble to anemone-form flowers sometimes marked with white. Vigorous, somewhat spreading plant with good foliage.

REG RAGLAND. E–L

Large, rich red, semidouble blossoms with smaller upright center petals surrounding yellow stamens. Slow, compact growth. There is a variegated form.

SHIRO CHAN. E–M

Sport of 'C. M. Wilson', hence a member of the Elegans tribe. Large, white, anemone-form flowers with a faint pink blush at petal bases.

SWAN LAKE. M–L

Large, white flowers ranging in form from formal double to loose peony form with yellow stamens interspersed. Vigorous, upright, with dense foliage.

TIFFANY. M

Large to very large, light pink flowers deepening toward petal edges; loose peony to anemone form. Strong, upright plant.

TINSIE. M

Miniature, anemone-form flower with a row of dark red guard petals surrounding a central mass of white petaloids. Plant is vigorous and upright. 'Bob's Tinsie' is similar, but flower is entirely red.

TOMORROW. E–M

Very large, bright red, semidouble with petaloids mixed in center to full peony form. Strong, open, somewhat pendulous growth. 'Tomorrow Varie-

TOP: 'Nuccio's Pearl'
CENTER: 'Pink Perfection'
BOTTOM: 'Ville de Nantes'

gated' has white markings. 'Tomorrow Park Hill' has light pink flowers deepening toward the edges, with some variegation. 'Tomorrow's Dawn' has pink flowers, with petals shading to white at the outer edges. 'Tomorrow's Tropic Dawn' has white flowers streaked with red and aging to blush.

VILLE DE NANTES. M–L

Sport of 'Donckelarii' and identical to it except that all the petals are fimbriated. Has proved subject to dieback in the South. H.

CAMELLIA RETICULATA

The word most often associated with *C. reticulata* is "spectacular." In size of both flower and plant, reticulatas are the largest: blooms may reach 9 inches across, and old Chinese records speak of ancient plants 50 feet tall.

Apart from their size, reticulata flowers are often distinguishable for the silky sheen of their petals as well. Colors vary from red through medium pink—some variegated with white—and newer varieties are extending the color range to lighter shades of pink and even white. Characteristically, these blossoms are semidouble with prominent stamens; in many varieties, some petals tend to fold and curl, standing up in "rabbit ear" fashion. A very few are fully double (formal double), rose form, or peony form.

Reticulatas are more open and tree-like than most japonicas, and reticulata foliage lacks the richness and glossiness of japonicas. These plants are also less free-flowering than japonicas, but compensate by the size of individual blossoms. Hardiness is variable, but most varieties don't perform well where winter minimum temperatures fall below 15°F/−9°C. These are favorite greenhouse plants in cool areas.

BUDDHA. M
Very large, rose pink, semidouble flowers with irregular, wavy petals and upstanding "rabbit ears." Strong, upright, open growth.

BUTTERFLY WINGS. M
Very large, rose pink, semidouble blooms with broad, wavy petals. Slender, open growth.

CAPTAIN RAWES. L
Very large, reddish rose pink, semidouble flowers with broad, wavy petals. Earliest reticulata introduced into cultivation (1820), and possibly the hardiest. Vigorous and bushy for a reticulata.

CHANG'S TEMPLE. M–L
Large, deep rose pink, open-centered semidouble blooms with deeply notched petals and a sprinkling of petaloids in the center. Vigorous, erect plant. Synonym: Cornelian

CHRYSANTHEMUM PETALS. M
Medium, light pink, rose-form to formal double flowers with fluted petals. Growth is open and slender.

CORNELIAN. M
Very large, rose pink to red flowers strongly marked with white; semidouble to peony form. Petals are wavy and crinkled. Vigorous and compact grower. Synonyms: 'Chang's Temple', 'Lion Head' (of which 'Cornelian' is a variegated form).

CRIMSON ROBE M–L
Very large, bright red, semidouble flowers with wavy, crinkled petals. Spreading, open plant, often with cream variegation on the foliage.

MOUTANCHA. L
Very large, brilliant pink, peony to formal double flowers with white veins and occasional stripes. Blooms resemble double peonies (the name is Chinese for "peony camellia").

PAGODA. M
Large, dark red, formal double to rose-form flower of great depth. Plant is compact (for a reticulata).

PROFESSOR TSAI. M–L
Medium, rose pink, semidouble flowers with undulating petals. Open, spreading growth habit.

PURPLE GOWN. M
Large, deep purplish red flowers with some white markings; formal purple double to peony form with wavy petals. Compact plant with attractive foliage and habit.

TOP: 'Buddha'
BOTTOM: 'Shot Silk'

SHOT SILK. M
Large, brilliant pink, loose semidouble flowers with iridescent, wavy petals. Vigorous, fast-growing plant.

TALI QUEEN. M
Very large, deep pink to red, semidouble blooms with irregular petals. Medium upright habit.

WHITE RETIC. L
Large, white, semidouble flowers with faint pink shading on petal reverse, opening from pink buds. Medium upright habit.

WILLIAM HERTRICH. M
Very large, cherry red, semidouble flowers with large, reflexed outer petals and smaller inner petals mixed with petaloids. Vigorous and bushy.

WILLOW WAND. M
Large, orchid pink, rose-form to semidouble flowers with irregular, wavy petals. Vigorous, erect, and narrow habit.

CAMELLIA SASANQUA

Varieties of *C. sasanqua* (and the closely related *C. hiemalis*) are the harbingers of camellia season. They begin blooming in chrysanthemum time—autumn—and are usually finished when the japonicas begin to take center stage.

Though the individual blossoms of most sasanquas are not as impressive or lasting as those of the reticulatas and many japonicas, sasanqua plants compensate by producing more blooms than other camellias—the sasanqua is truly the azalea of the camellia world. Flowers include the full range of color and all flower forms.

All plants listed below are sold as sasanquas, although some carry characteristics transferred from *C. japonica* and are known as hiemalis sasanquas. Those designated as *C. vernalis* are hybrids between *C. sasanqua* and *C. japonica*.

APPLE BLOSSOM. E–M

🌺 Small, white, single flowers with pink blush. Growth is vigorous, upright, somewhat spreading.

CHANSONETTE. M–L

🌺 Medium, deep pink, formal double flowers open to show a yellow center. Plant is bushy, but with long, limber branches. A hiemalis sasanqua variety.

CHOJI GURUMA. E–M

🌺 Medium, light pink, anemone-form flowers with deeper shading toward tips of petals and petaloids. Upright, somewhat narrow growth.

CLEOPATRA. E–M

🌺 Small, rose pink, semidouble flowers with narrow petals. Upright, compact growth; useful for hedges.

HANA JIMAN. E–M

🌺 Large, white, semidouble flowers with fluted petals edged in pink. Upright, vigorous, compact growth.

HIRYU. L

🌺 Small, deep red, double flowers on a compact plant. Blooms in fall with sasanquas. Technically a variety of *C. vernalis*. 'Hiryu Nishiki' is variegated with white.

JEAN MAY. E–M

🌺 Large, shell pink, double blossoms on an upright, compact plant with glossy leaves. Protect flowers from hottest sun.

KANJIRO. M–L

🌺 Large, rose red, single to semidouble flowers with fluted petals. Plant is tall, dense, with glossy foliage. Good hedge plant. Synonym: 'Australian Hiryu'. A hiemalis sasanqua variety.

MINE-NO-YUKI. E–M

🌺 Small, white, semidouble to peony-form flowers. Spreading, willowy growth. Splendid espalier plant. Commonly known as 'White Doves'.

NARUMI-GATA.. E–M

🌺 Large, white, cup-shaped, single flowers, shaded pink. Compact, upright plant.

SETSUGEKKA. E–M

🌺 Large, white, semidouble with fluted petals. Vigorous, upright, somewhat open growth.

SHISHI-GASHIRA. M–L

🌺 Medium, rose red, semidouble to double flowers over a 5-month season. Low, arching growth. Can take full sun. Valuable landscape plant for ground cover, trailing over walls, foundation planting. A hiemalis sasanqua variety.

SHOWA-NO-SAKAE. M–L

🌺 Medium large, soft pink, semidouble to rose-form flowers. Fast growing, willowy, arching. Superb hanging basket plant. 'Showa Supreme' is similar, but with peony-form flowers. Both are hiemalis sasanqua varieties.

TANYA. E–M

🌺 Small, deep rose pink, single flowers. Low growing, spreading. Good ground cover variety.

YULETIDE. L

🌺 Small, bright red, single flowers with an orange undertone. Plant is narrow, dense, and erect. Flowering is heavy in midwinter—around Christmas—and may continue until spring.

TOP: 'Jean May'
CENTER: 'Mine-No-Yuki'
BOTTOM: 'Yuletide'

EXTRA-HARDY CAMELLIAS

These camellias have proved exceptionally cold-hardy and are well worth trying in locations east and south of a line from Richmond to Baltimore to Long Island. They are of three sorts: *C. japonica* varieties bred for cold tolerance; hybrids involving *C. oleifera* and *C. sasanqua*, which are fall blooming; and hybrids of *C. oleifera* and *C. japonica*, which bloom in the spring.

SPRING-BLOOMING *C. JAPONICA* SELECTIONS 'April Blush', shell pink; 'April Dawn', pink-and-white variegated; 'April Kiss', red; 'April Remembered', cream- to pink-shaded; 'April Rose', rose red; 'April Snow', white; 'April Tryst', red.

FALL-BLOOMING HYBRIDS BETWEEN *C. OLEIFERA* AND *C. SASANQUA* OR *C. HIEMALIS* (hardy to –10°F/–23°C in extremely protected sites) 'Polar Ice', white; 'Snow Flurry', white; 'Winter's Beauty', shell pink with very light pink petaloids; 'Winter's Charm', lavender pink; 'Winter's Dream', pink; 'Winter's Fire', rose pink; 'Winter's Hope', white; 'Winter's Interlude', pink; 'Winter's Peony', medium to light pink; 'Winter's Rose', shell pink; 'Winter's Star', light purplish red; 'Winter's Waterlily', white.

SPRING-BLOOMING HYBRIDS BETWEEN *C. OLEIFERA* AND *C. JAPONICA* 'Betty Sette', pink; 'Fire n Ice', deep dark red and white; 'Ice Follies', medium to light rose pink; 'Pink Icicle', shell pink; 'Spring Icicle', bright pink.

HYBRID CAMELLIAS

Interspecies hybridization of camellias was predicted 150 years ago, but the actual practice began around the time of World War II. The first hybrids were introduced in 1940, and the pace of hybridization accelerated thereafter. It continues today. The first crosses were made in England between *C. japonica* and *C. saluenensis*, a Chinese species introduced in 1917; these plants are called *C. williamsii* after the man who first made these crosses. Later, *C. sasanqua* and *C. reticulata* were thrown into the gene pool, where they continue to contribute floriferousness and flower size.

The results, typified by 'Donation' and 'J. C. Williams', were rather japonica-like plants with a profusion of medium-size pink flowers. Further and more diverse breeding have produced a larger, more varied group of hybrids notable for an abundance of flowers over a long period, early bloom, better performance in sunny locations, and blooms that range from orchid to nearly lavender in color. In general, these hybrids are vigorous, bushy growers—attractive shrubs throughout the year.

Today, other camellia species are being used to further desirable traits. The species *C. oleifera*, possibly the hardiest of all camellias, has proved a useful parent for producing cold-tolerant offspring. Fragrance is yet another trait that hybridizers are striving for, with crosses with *C. lutchuensis* and others. For flower size, hybridizers are turning to *C. granthamiana*.

Yellow-flowered camellia species have remained frustratingly out of reach for breeders: they are native to strife-torn and politically inaccessible northern Indochina. But the year 1980, when the first plants of the yellow *C. chrysantha* from Vietnam were raised from seed in the United States, may have marked a turning point in camellia development.

Another plant within the camellia family is *C. sinensis*, or tea. Flowers of the tea plant are small, profuse, and usually white, but the plant is grown for its leaves. Plants are dense in habit, with small, net-veined leaves, and can be clipped into dense cushions or planted as a low hedge.

The hardiness of these cultivars is extremely variable and many have not been tried in colder areas. Hybrids between *C. japonica* and *C. saluenensis* are reasonably hardy, as are any hybrids with *C. oleifera*. Hybrids with *C. reticulata*, *C. granthamiana*, or *C. chrysantha* (*C. nitidissima*) are generally less hardy. Before attempting to grow varieties on this list in colder areas, consult an experienced camellia grower.

CALIFORNIA DAWN. E–M
Sasanqua-reticulata hybrid. Large, light pink, semidouble to loose peony-form flowers, with crinkled petals. Vigorous, upright, bushy plant. The same cross has produced 'California Sunrise', an early bloomer with blush pink rabbit-ear semidouble flowers on a somewhat open bush; and 'California Sunset', another early bloomer, with large, deep rose pink, semidouble flowers with wavy petals.

CHINA LADY. E–M
Reticulata-granthamiana cross. Very large, deep orchid pink, irregular semidouble flowers. Growth is open, and foliage narrow and net-veined, as with the *C. granthamiana* parent.

CORAL DELIGHT. M
Saluenensis-japonica hybrid. Medium, rich coral pink, semidouble flowers sometimes with white markings. Medium, upright, compact plant with small, dark green leaves.

DONATION. M
Saluenensis-japonica cross. Large, orchid pink, semidouble blooms freely produced on a compact, spreading plant. One of the earliest

hybrid camellias. 'Donation Variegated' has flowers marbled with white. H.

DR. CLIFFORD PARKS. M

Reticulata-japonica cross. Very large, rich red, semidouble to peony- or anemone-form flowers. Vigorous, upright plant.

E. G. WATERHOUSE. M–L

Saluenensis-japonica cross. Medium, light pink, formal double flowers heavily produced on a strong, columnar plant. There is a variegated form. Probably hardy.

FLOWER GIRL. M

Sasanqua-reticulata cross. Large to very large, bright pink, semidouble to peony-form flowers heavily produced along the branches of a vigorous, upright plant.

FRANCIE L. M–L

Saluenensis-reticulata cross. Very large, rose pink, semidouble flowers with high centers and irregular, wavy petals. There is a variegated form.

FREEDOM BELL. E–M

Japonica cross. Small, bright red, bell-shaped semidouble flowers. Growth is medium, upright, somewhat rangy. Long bloom period. Probably hardy.

HIGH FRAGRANCE. M–L

Japonica-lutchuensis cross. Medium, pale ivory pink, peony-form flowers, deeper pink at petal edges; sweet scent. Vigorous, open growth.

HONEYMOON. L

Japonica-pitardii-chrysantha cross. Medium to large, creamy white, semidouble flowers, with yellow at the bases of the petals. Flowers buds are pink. Vigorous, open, upright growth.

HOWARD ASPER. M–L

Reticulata-japonica cross. Very large, salmon pink, loose peony-form flowers. Large, spreading plant with handsome, large foliage.

J. C. WILLIAMS. M–L

Saluenensis-japonica cross. Medium, pink, cup-shaped single flowers. Vigorous, erect plant with somewhat pendulous branches. Named for the first successful breeder of hybrid camellias. H.

JOE NUCCIO. E–L

Williamsii-japonica cross. Medium, orchid pink, formal double with incurved petal tips tinted deeper pink. Very long bloom season. Upright, bushy plant. Probably hardy.

JURY'S YELLOW. E–L

Japonica-saluenensis hybrid. Medium, anemone-form flowers with outer petals of ivory white and a large central puff of creamy yellow feathery petaloids. Compact, upright growth.

LEONARD MESSEL. M

Reticulata-saluenensis-japonica hybrid. Large, rose pink, semidouble flowers with wavy petals. Vigorous, upright, open plant.

MARY CHRISTIAN. M

Japonica-saluenensis hybrid. Resembles 'Donation', but flowers are deeper pink, somewhat bell-shaped, and pendent.

SCENTED SUN. M

Lutchuensis-japonica hybrid. Large to very large, pink-striped white, irregular semidouble flowers with flared stamens. Occasional flowers are solid pink or rose. Vigorous, erect growth.

TOP: 'China Lady'
CENTER: 'Donation'
BOTTOM: 'Freedom Bell'

VALENTINE DAY. M

Reticulata-japonica cross. Large to very large, salmon pink, formal double flowers. Plant is medium-slow growing, upright.

VALLEY KNUDSEN. M–L

Saluenensis-reticulata cross. Large to very large, deep orchid pink, semidouble to loose peony-form flowers. Plant growth is erect, compact.

For azaleas, rhododendrons, and camellias, spring is the main event. It is then that you'll see some of the most heavily flowering evergreens on the planet, and then that you'll see

SECRETS OF
SUCCESS

deciduous azaleas fill our woodlands with their spring fire. The secret to creating this glory in your own garden is simply to give the plants what they need to thrive. Once you learn their basic requirements, you'll find that keeping your azaleas, rhododendrons, and camellias in good health is no more difficult than maintaining any other plants in your garden.

Azaleas, rhododendrons, and camellias are generally grouped together because their basic needs are similar. They like a rich, moist, acidic soil that drains well; shelter from wind and direct sun; and a cool, humid atmosphere. If you're lucky, your garden will duplicate these conditions. But even if it doesn't, you can use plenty of tricks to create a microclimate where your plants will flourish. Just turn the page to get started.

Given the right growing conditions and some basic care, azaleas, rhododendrons, and camellias will reward you with spring color.

Getting Started

Whatever you hope to achieve in your garden, the process usually begins in a retail nursery. You find yourself standing in a lath house surrounded by scores of fully flowering azaleas, rhododendrons, and camellias in all sizes and price ranges. And you wonder, "Where do I begin?"

BEGIN WITH WHAT YOU HAVE

If there's a good starting rule of thumb for buying plants, it's this: buy only plants that will complement—not compete with—the plants around them. Consider five key factors—flower color and form, foliage, habit, and size, as well as hardiness—to ensure that the plant you buy has all the qualities you want for your garden.

Also think about bloom time and duration. Some landscape architects think of rhododendrons as designer plants: you can pick just about any combination of size, habit, color, and leaf texture you want, then find a rhododendron to fill the bill. Bear in mind that rhododendrons tend to flower all at once, going from first to last bloom in 3 weeks or so. If you want a longer bloom season, plant early-, mid-, and late-season varieties, but match plants to your climate: if you live in a place where hard frosts come late, early rhododendron flowers may be frozen off before you can enjoy them.

Camellias have a narrower color range, but set against their deep green, glossy foliage, the flowers convey a purity and perfection found in few other plants. Each plant also blooms over a longer period than its rhododendron counterparts: some of the best camellias keep flowering for 2 to 3 months.

FLOWER COLOR AND FORM. Rhododendrons come in every color except sky blue, and breeders are undoubtedly working on that. Nurseries often group named varieties by color, with labels noting when each variety blooms—early, mid-, or late season. Flowers can be bell- or funnel-shaped, single or double, ruffled or not. They usually combine to form trusses that are huge and round, but sometimes they're loose and open. Because flower quality is as variable as type among rhododendrons, number ratings are often assigned, along with ratings for plant appearance and performance (see page 36 for an explanation of these ratings).

Camellias come mostly in whites, pinks, and rose reds. A good yellow camellia *(C. chrysantha)* exists, but so far breeders haven't had much luck passing its golden yellow genes into

Well-stocked retail nurseries offer a large plant selection and a range of sizes.

large-flowering hybrids. They've come up with some pleasing pale yellows, but there's clearly more work to be done. Still, the camellia's colors are nothing to weep about: breeders have produced endless combinations of stripes, speckles, marbling, edging, and shading.

What camellias lack in color range, they make up for in flower form. Different varieties call to mind anemones, roses, peonies—even water lilies and hibiscus. (For a look at designated flower forms, see the illustrations on page 61.) Another difference is that some camellias, like the Japanese Higos, have stamens clustered as densely as hairs on a paintbrush, while others hide them entirely.

FOLIAGE. First, remember something most plant breeders learn early in their careers: you live with the flowers for a few weeks per year, and the plant for 52 weeks. Buy something with a nice-looking shape and a dense mass of foliage—perhaps a plant whose leaves will contrast nicely with the coarser or finer foliage of its neighbors in the garden.

As you choose rhododendrons or azaleas, use all your senses. Big-leafed rhododendrons are impressive to look at (*R. sinogrande* leaves can be 20 inches long and half as wide), while fine-leafed rhododendrons often have fragrant foliage: brush your hand across *R. augustinii* and you'll smell balsam. Try the same thing with a Mollis azalea's fresh new foliage and you may smell a skunk. Though they're the exception, some camellia and rhododendron flowers even have fragrance—as do many deciduous azaleas. Sniff before you buy.

Deciduous azaleas and some evergreens can show smashing fall leaf color; other plants have new growth with startling geometry. Some, such as *R. yakushimanum* varieties, have a feltlike layer called *indumentum* on the underside of each leaf that may be a different color. Touching it is like feeling the inside of a rabbit's ear.

Of all the different kinds of camellias, almost everybody likes the glossy green leaves of the japonicas, but the reticulatas are interesting, too. Their matte green, netted leaves make a good foil for their flowers.

HABIT. Most camellias have a fairly upright habit. Rhododendrons, however, have a wide range of growth habits: some are trailing, others make perfect little domes, and a few are quite open. Often these tendencies are difficult to discern in 1- or 2-gallon containers. Somebody needs to tell you how the plants will grow—in other words, shop at a place where the staff really knows the plants, or check your references, starting with this book, before you buy. Plant tags may also help.

SIZE. Again, this is a no-brainer in a good nursery, a mystery in a bad one. Ask how big your prospective plant will grow in 10 years, and how well it takes to pruning. As with color and habit, mature size varies more among rhododendrons than among camellias. Some full-grown rhododendrons are barely more than ground covers, while others become flowering trees. Most camellias can eventually grow house-high, but they take well to pruning, so you can keep the plants to just head-high without much trouble.

HARDINESS. Most retail nurseries sell only what grows well locally, but some sell plants of borderline hardiness; their notion is that experienced gardeners like to push the limits of what they can grow, using microclimates and frost-protection schemes to nurse tender plants through tough winters. Before you buy, ask whether the plant you have your eye on is hardy enough to handle the worst winter of the decade. If you order plants by mail, you'll have to depend on hardiness zone maps and plant descriptions to decide whether a given plant would be a good bet in your garden.

WHEN TO BUY

When to buy your plants depends a lot on where you buy them. Retail garden centers do the most business when plants are in full flower, so that's when they have the greatest selection. Mail-order sources want to sell when plants are dormant and the season is cool, because that's when plants are most tolerant of stress due to shipping.

RETAIL NURSERIES AND GARDEN CENTERS. By purchasing shrubs in flower—that is, if they're old enough to bloom—you see exactly what you're getting. That's an advantage over buying shrubs sight unseen, since colors do vary, occasionally even within the same named varieties, and especially over each flower's individual life (some blooms age to darker or lighter shades).

You can buy containerized plants just about any day of the year, but it's easiest on both you and the shrub if you buy and plant during mild weather. If you live in a hot-summer, mild-winter climate, fall planting will probably give you the highest rate of success, because plants will have plenty of time to establish roots before spring bloom and the following summer's wilting heat. However, if you live in a place where most winters are hard enough for the ground to freeze, plant in early spring so that plants will be well established by the following winter.

MAIL ORDER. The mail-order nurseries listed on page 75 offer a seemingly endless array of plants and scions (cuttings you can graft onto your own plants). All are thoroughly described in each firm's mail-order catalog. The photographs are always fetching, but be aware that the photographic film often skews flower colors; those in the purple-blue end of the spectrum, for example, shade toward magenta.

Different mail-order operations have different policies: some ship year-round, while others ship only when plants are either dormant (in the case of deciduous rhododendrons and azaleas) or after the foliage is hardened off and before the next year's new growth comes on (August through March). Most don't ship to frigid areas in midwinter, or to hot parts of the country in August, but check when you order. Nobody wants frozen or fried plants showing up on the doorstep.

CHOOSING HEALTHY STOCK

When you buy mail-order stock, you're at the mercy of the sender; on the other hand, established mail-order nurseries simply don't last if they send out inferior plants. Plants they ship will probably be on the small side and rooted in lightweight soil, since heavy, large plants are too costly to ship.

Some azaleas and rhododendrons will reward you with fragrance.

When you shop, pick the source before you pick the plant. One outstanding wholesale grower complained about the fate of many plants he sold to retailers who just sideline in seasonal nursery stock: some plants were sold from parking-lots, where they fried in hot weather. Plants need the kind of care good nursery people can give them, so shop with people whose business is to sell plants. Nurseries and garden centers are good places to start.

After you've selected the variety you want, spend some extra time choosing the pick of the litter. Get a plant that has several branches breaking out to the sides—not one that has one or two leafy, unbranched sticks growing out of the soil—and obviously healthy foliage. Slide it out of the container to check the roots: the tips should be white, and not spiraling around the inside of the pot.

Camellias flower young, so many 1-gallon plants and most 2-gallon or larger plants will be flowering if you buy them in season. Avoid plants with scale insects (see "Sooty Mold" on page 108), whose honeylike droppings coat leaves and bring on sooty mold.

Some rhododendron hybrids flower by the time they're 2 years old, and most by 4 years, but a few others take much longer. Loderi rhododendrons, for example, can take 8 years to flower. Expect a well-grown, 4-year-old blooming rhododendron to have a 10- to 15-inch spread and plenty of branches. A commercial grower can produce a larger rhododendron faster by not pinching its branch tips back, but such a plant looks like a

This large *Rhododendron calophytum* was successfully transplanted in its new home.

poorly branched stick in a pot; it's not what you want. Go for density, perhaps three or four major branches within a few inches of the soil, and even (not lopsided) form.

As you shop, look for mildewed leaves, which show up on some kinds of rhododendrons in the Pacific Northwest and deciduous azaleas everywhere, especially in autumn. Some mildew is to be expected on most kinds of deciduous azaleas right at season's end, but avoid plants with really bad cases. Mildewed evergreen rhododendrons, which have brown leaf patches all year, are more of a problem. Don't buy a plant that has it.

Whatever you buy, it helps to get a replacement guarantee. It warrants the plant to be free of insects and disease, and protects you from plants that are extremely pot-bound or that might have broken or chopped-off roots; you, of course, have to feed and water the plants faithfully if you hope to collect on the guarantee.

HOW PLANTS ARE SOLD

Camellias (and most other nursery plants) are sold by the size container they come in. The most common are 1 gallon (also called 6 inch, for the container's diameter), 2 gallon (8 inch), 3 gallon (10 inch), 4 gallon (11 inch), and 5 gallon (12 inch).

Rhododendrons and azaleas are often sold by the width of the canopy instead. You'll find 12- to 15-inch, 15- to 18-inch, and 18- to 24-inch plants in most nurseries. Prices are often determined by the inch: a 24-inch rhododendron, for example, might be sold for $1 an inch, or $24.

If you buy plants whose rootballs are wrapped in burlap (balled and burlapped, or "B and B" for short), peel the burlap back and have a look at the rootball. It should be held firmly together by a network of fibrous roots. If you encounter major broken roots, or if soil sloughs away to reveal a much smaller rootball, look for another plant.

Many nurseries also sell field-grown plants. They dig them and wrap the roots in plastic or burlap for the trip home. These are usually excellent deals, especially if you keep the time between digging and transplanting short.

TOP: Rhododendron **indumentum**
BOTTOM: Rhododendrons sold in containers

Shopping For Azaleas, Rhododendrons, Camellias

When you're looking for azaleas, rhododendrons, and camellias, you may find that local nurseries carry a wide selection of plants that do well in your region. But if you're looking for a specific species or hybrid, a nursery specializing in these plants may be your best source. The following growers publish catalogs or price lists and can ship plants to you.

BOVEES NURSERY
1737 S.W. Coronado St.
Portland, OR 97219
(503) 244-9341
(800) 435-9250
www.bovees.com
bovees@teleport.com
Vireyas and common rhododendrons

CARLSON'S GARDENS
P.O. Box 305
South Salem, NY 10590
(914) 763-5958
bigazaleas@aol.com
Hardy azaleas and rhododendrons; catalog and color card $3

GIRARD'S NURSERIES
P.O. Box 428
Geneva, OH 44041
(440) 466-2881
Hardy azaleas and rhododendrons

GOSSLER FARMS NURSERY
1200 Weaver Road
Springfield, OR 97478-9691
(541) 746-3922
Rhododendrons, camellias, and companion plants; catalog $2

GREER GARDENS
1280 Goodpasture Island Road
Eugene, OR 97401
(541) 686-8266
Azaleas, rhododendrons, camellias, and a wide variety of companion plants; catalog $3

KELLEYGREEN NURSERY
P.O. Box 1130
Drain, OR 97435
(800) 477-5676
Rhododendrons, azaleas, and companion plants

NUCCIO'S NURSERIES
3555 Chaney Trail
Altadena, CA 91001
Mailing Address:
P.O. Box 6160
Altadena, CA 91103
(626) 794-3383
Camellias and azaleas

PUSHEPETAPPA GARDENS
2317 Washington St.
Franklinton, LA 70438
(504) 839-4930
Azaleas, rhododendrons, and camellias; catalog $1

RAREFINDNURSERY
957 Patterson Road
Jackson, NJ 08527
(732) 833-0613
Hardy rhododendrons, azaleas, and companion plants; catalog $1

ROSLYN NURSERY
211 Burrs Lane
Dix Hills, NY 11746
(516) 643-9347
Azaleas, rhododendrons, and camellias; catalog $3

A SANDY RHODODENDRON
www.rhodo.com
Rhododendron selection

SEAVIEW, INC.
4329 Chrisella Road East
Puyallup, WA 96372
(253) 845-8043
(253) 845-1678 (fax)
FTMinch@aol.com
Seeds for rhododendrons and azaleas

SHEPHERD HILL FARM
200 Peekskill Hollow Road
Putnam Valley, NY 10579-3217
WXGL87B@prodigy.com
Hardy evergreen azaleas and hardy rhododendrons

HULYN SMITH
Valdosta Camellias
2436 Meadowbrook Drive
Valdosta, GA 31602-1207
(912) 242-1390
Camellia cuttings only

WAYSIDE GARDENS
1 Garden Lane
Hodges, SC 29695
(800) 845-1124
(800) 817-1124 (fax)
Large plant selection

WHITNEY RHODODENDRON GARDENS AND NURSERY
P.O. Box F
Brinnon, WA 98320
(360) 796-4411
(800) 952-2404
Rhododendrons, camellias, and azaleas; catalog $4

Planting azaleas and rhododendrons under companion trees creates a microclimate they can thrive in.

SELECTING A PLANTING SITE

When you're deciding where to plant azaleas, camellias, and rhododendrons, you'll want to satisfy both your taste in garden design and the plants' needs for the right site and microclimate. The good news is that plants tend to look best in the settings that help them grow best. Most azaleas, rhododendrons, and camellias are attractive in filtered shade under tall trees—just where many of them grow in the wild. Some design and site selection guidelines apply generally to azaleas, camellias, and rhododendrons. In addition, each plant group has its own likes and dislikes.

As you survey your garden, think about the soil in each prospective planting site, and avoid places where it doesn't drain well. Most azaleas, rhododendrons, and camellias simply won't survive waterlogged roots. Fortunately, unless soil problems are severe, they can be overcome when planting (see "Planting in Problem Soils" on page 84). Remember that all these shrubs root along the surface, and generally don't like to compete with the roots of other plants. Don't plant them beneath trees that have aggressive surface roots (see "Overstory Trees Your Shrubs Will Love—or Hate" on page 79).

There's spirited debate about whether to allow ground covers to grow over the roots of azaleas, rhododendrons, and camellias. Some large public gardens do it with success. The ground covers are allowed to ramble over the rhododendron roots, but as the rhododendrons and azaleas grow, they often shade the ground covers out. One camellia curator allows violets and dwarf mondo grass to grow over camellia roots—again with no problems for the camellia.

THE DESIGNER'S EYE

One of the most important considerations is how a given location will affect the impact of the flowers. An accomplished landscape designer once described what he did with red rhododendrons this way: "I mass them way out across the back lawn where they can shout back at me." That's not a bad strategy for red azaleas and camellias either. Bright colors really stand out when the sun shines.

In the evening, it's a different story altogether: reds and purples tend to go gray or disappear in twilight, while whites and shell pinks show well in moonlight and catch reflected garden lights. If you're one of those people who ends the workday with a stroll in the garden or a little predarkness watering and weeding, lighter-flowered plants can make your evening garden a dazzler. Plant them where you're most likely to see them at dusk: perhaps around the patio or along entry paths.

Flowers with intricate bloom patterns—bicolors and variegated blossoms, for example—are also best seen up close. Plant them by an entry, or just outside a dining room window. Keep fragrant plants in close as well: by the door, along a pathway, or in a patio planter box.

AIR FLOW

During the growing season, air tends to flow from the ocean onto the land during the day (right) and from the land back to the sea in the evening (far right). Prevailing breezes are intensified in canyons and in narrow passages that lie parallel to the wind. Winds can also speed up as they pass between two houses, creating a wind tunnel.

A WORD ABOUT MICROCLIMATES

There's a story about an old Japanese garden designer who started every job the same way: by sitting on the property for a full day. As the hours passed, he noted where the sun rose and set, which spots took the brunt of the afternoon's heat, and where prevailing winds came from. He used his imagination as well, thinking about the changing slant of the sun through the seasons, and how things would look when overstory trees were in leaf or out.

He was learning the site's microclimates—a sensible thing for anyone to do who wants to plant a garden. Azaleas, rhododendrons, and camellias all have their preferences. Give them conditions similar to those they encounter in the wild, and you'll probably succeed. Shoehorn them into a bad environment, and the plants won't satisfy you.

As you assess your own site, think about what makes some parts of your garden warmer, colder, or windier than other parts. Then think about how these things change from day to night and season to season.

SUNLIGHT. On winter's short days the sun rides low across the southern sky, while on the long days of summer it rides high. As you consider where to plant, think about where the shadows will fall during the hot months, when the sun is higher overhead during the heat of the day. For azaleas, rhododendrons, and camellias to perform best, they need plenty of light to produce abundant flowers, but in hot-summer climates, it's helpful to give all of them—especially rhododendrons—protection during the hottest hours of the day.

The more sunny days you have and the more extreme your climate, the more sun protection your plants will need. The milder your climate and the more summer fog and clouds you have, the more sun your plants will tolerate.

COLD POCKETS. Because cold air is heavy, it flows downhill, pooling in low places and backing up behind obstacles such as hedges, fences, and houses. These areas become frost pockets. On clear, still nights, flat, treeless pieces of ground also lose their heat quickly in a process called radiation heat loss, another invitation to frost.

Using that knowledge, you can predict where the frosty parts of the garden will be, or just go outside on a 32°F/0°C morning and look at where frost has formed during the night and where it hasn't. Plant tender shrubs in the frostless places—usually on sloping land where flowing cold air constantly mixes with nearby warmer air—or under trees.

EXPOSURE. Slopes that fall away to the south or west get more daytime heat than those that drop away to the north or northeast. If you live in the northern tier of the United States, that extra heat can hurt plants of borderline hardiness by prematurely forcing them out of dormancy. If you live in hotter climates farther south, you can temper the heat by planting on north- or east-facing slopes.

In the same way, walls reflect extra heat onto plants on their south and west sides, but offer shelter to plants growing on their north and east sides. These microclimates work in the same way as the slopes described above.

WIND. During the growing season, air tends to flow from the ocean onto the land during the day, and from the land back to sea in the evening. Breezes are intensified in canyons and valleys, and in long, narrow passages (between two houses or parallel rows of trees, for example) that lie along the direction of the wind.

Prevailing winds are often seasonal. Cold winter winds are usually the most damaging to broad-leafed evergreens such as azaleas, rhododendrons, and camellias, because they can dry out plants so quickly. Freezing soil is doubly damaging because it prevents surface roots from taking in moisture to replace what's lost through the leaves.

You can divert cold winds by planting a windbreak. In fact, the most important part of your azalea, rhododendron, and camellia collection could be a row of conifers that shelters the plants from the biting winds of winter. That shelter belt will also make a great background for the flowers your azaleas, camellias, and rhododendrons will give you in winter and spring.

COLD AIR POCKETS

Cold air drains

Cold air pools here

Cold air flows downhill like water, and "puddles" in basins. So a sunken planting area may leave your plants shivering, even when higher or more protected surroundings are balmy.

HOW A WINDBREAK WORKS

Windbreaks divert the wind, creating pockets that protect plants from wind damage. Trees and shrubs used as windbreaks can protect an area that stretches behind them for up to 8 times their height.

RHODODENDRONS: FROM DRIPPING MOUNTAIN FORESTS TO YOUR GARDEN

When plant explorers started searching for rhododendrons in the eastern Himalayas, they hit the mother lode. These mountains—which rise between Burma, southwest China, and eastern Nepal—are packed with rhododendron species. Because the rainfall level is high there, the soil is acid and plant roots almost never dry out. The rains also keep things cool in summer, while snows and forest trees insulate plants from biting cold winter winds. As the thick mulch of dead leaves slowly breaks down, mycorrhizal fungi help rhododendron roots extract the nutrients they need from the loose, highly organic soil.

In a garden, most rhododendrons want pretty much the same thing that they find on their own: regular watering year-round, acid soil, protection from extremely hot or cold weather, and good drainage. As for the mycorrhiza, don't worry: it will probably come with the plants you buy.

The ideal environment for growing rhododendrons is open woodland, where tall trees filter the sunlight and shelter plants from wind, frost, and excessive heat. You may not have a woodland in your garden, but you probably have a few trees to supply the shelter that rhododendrons thrive under. Tall trees pruned high provide perfect filtered light for them. In contrast, trees with low canopies force rhododendrons to stretch to the sides to get light, and they quickly lose their natural shapes.

Shelter from summer sun is less important the farther north you garden. In the Pacific Northwest, that principle holds absolutely: rhododendrons grow splendidly there in open sun, and it's not unusual to see house-high rhododendrons trained as bare-trunked flowering trees. In winter, however, rhododendrons growing at the same latitudes in cold-winter parts of the country need the shelter of overarching trees to provide that extra bit of protection against frost.

One last rule of thumb will help you site your plants in the garden: Lower-growing rhododendrons and

Azaleas look right at home in a Japanese garden.

those whose leaves are silvery, smaller, or more leathery can usually take more sun than taller, larger-leafed kinds. Many of the dwarfs are also wonderful little plants on their own merits: they can transform a rockery or tiny entry garden.

AZALEAS: MORE FLOWERS, MORE ADAPTABILITY

Azaleas are a complex tribe. It's hard to generalize about their native ranges because they're such a mixed lot. In broad terms, however, they can tolerate hotter, drier conditions than rhododendrons.

These plants look especially good when planted in masses. Think of most azaleas as plants of the forest edge. The country's most beautiful gardens usually plant azaleas in borders that are backed by trees and fronted by lawns. It's not a bad idea to plant them fairly close together initially, then dig them and move them farther apart as they mature (see "Transplanting Basics" on page 84).

Deciduous azaleas generally thrive in the northern tier of the United States. Many of them have good fall color—if mildew doesn't spoil it.

Different kinds prefer different locations in the garden. Northern Lights hybrids, for example, are hardy enough ($-45°F/-43°C$) to prosper in the garden's cold spots. Mollis hybrids like full sun, whereas royal azalea *(R. schlippenbachii)* does best in filtered light. And if you have a damp spot in the garden with no standing water, try Viscosum hybrids, which have swamp azaleas in the family tree.

Evergreen azaleas are in their prime along the entire West Coast, in the South, and through the mid-Atlantic states. Some selected varieties do well even into Ontario, Canada, but they're definitely pushing the envelope. Expect evergreen azaleas to lose most of their leaves in hard winters and in the northern parts of their ranges. Even in more temperate climates, most evergreen azaleas barely qualify as such: they lose their old leaves just after new leaves come on in spring.

Smaller azaleas make excellent rock garden plants.

In most cases, evergreen azaleas can handle more heat than deciduous kinds, and Southern Indicas have greater sun tolerance. But there are some important caveats. Orange- and pastel-colored flowers often fade badly in full sun, and the Kurume azaleas are clearly happiest in filtered sun. Rhododendron rules also apply here: plants growing in milder climates and more northerly latitudes can tolerate more sun.

CAMELLIAS: COOL-SEASON COLOR AT ITS BEST

Like their distant rhododendron relations, many of the camellias are shrubs and trees of the open forest, although one of the most popular *(Camellia japonica)* is native to the coastal scrublands of Japan, Korea, and China. Most camellias live where summers are wet and winters are cool and on the dry side.

Almost all kinds of *C. japonica, C. reticulata,* and *C. sasanqua* also take full sun in most areas. But if you live in a hot-summer, mild-winter climate, give plants a spot in the garden that's in at least partial shade during the warmest midday hours. Also, keep their roots cool by retaining the shrub's lower leaves instead of pruning the plant into tree form.

If you plant camellias under trees, make sure the trees are high branched and deep rooted. Dense, low-branched trees cast too much shade, which inhibits camellia bud set. Oaks are near perfect overstory hosts, with one group of exceptions. West Coast native oaks need dry summers to survive, while camellias need plenty of summer water. If you put the two too close together, you may end up killing the oak (a 10- or 15-year process) to keep the camellia from dying of thirst. Keep the camellia out of the oak's root zone, preferably on the tree's north or east side.

Most camellias also take well to training, particularly good news if you garden in a rainy-winter climate. You can espalier an early bloomer like *C. sasanqua* flat against a trellis under the eaves of your house, and keep rain from knocking the flowers apart and settings up conditions for camellia petal blight.

All camellias like to be kept out of cold winds, which damage early flowers—especially light pinks and whites. The *C. williamsii* hybrids, made by crossing *C. saluenensis* with *C. japonica,* suffer the least damage from the weather, even in their lighter color range, and are excellent varieties for the mild northern latitudes of the Pacific Northwest.

If you live along the northern edge of camellia country (on a line from St. Louis to New York, then north along the coast), you'll need to pull out all the stops to get bloom: plant one of the extra-hardy varieties (see "Extra-Hardy Camellias" on page 68), give it overhead frost protection, shelter it from cold winds, and site it in a south or west exposure, where it will get extra warmth. Most years you should get the camellias you want.

In any climate, plant camellias where they won't get the morning's first sun, which can mark them with light brown spots and also cause frosty buds to open unevenly or not at all.

This camellia is protected from leaf-spotting rain while also it camouflages a downspout.

OVERSTORY TREES YOUR SHRUBS WILL LOVE— OR HATE

Overstory trees have many advantages for azaleas, rhododendrons, and camellias, but not all trees are equally hospitable to the plants that grow beneath them. The following recommendations assume well-drained soil that is reasonably deep; shallow soils can force even good trees to root along the surface, where they'll compete with your shrubs.

In the wild, many azaleas and rhododendrons grow among conifers. The Pacific Northwest is full of gorgeous rhododendron gardens planted among Douglas firs, but not right next to them, where it's bone dry. Rhododendrons and camellias can grow that way in your garden as well. Just make sure to plant them outside the trees' drip lines: many conifers are surface rooted, and many also drop limbs in high wind, breaking apart plants below. Let the trees' height, rather than their canopy, give plants the shade they need.

GOOD TREES WITH DEEP ROOTS
DOGWOOD *(Cornus)*
KATSURA TREE *(Cercidiphyllum japonicum)*
OAKS—*(Quercus)* most
PINES—*(Pinus)* most
SILVER BELL *(Halesia)*
SNOWBELL *(Styrax)*
SOUR GUM *(Nyssa sylvatica)*

PROBLEM TREES WITH AGGRESSIVE ROOTS OR OVERLY DENSE TOPS
ASH *(Fraxinus)*
BEECH *(Fagus)*
BIRCH *(Betula)*
ELM *(Ulmus)*
LINDEN *(Tilia)*
MAPLES—*(Acer)* many
POPLAR *(Populus)*
PIN OAK *(Quercus palustris)*
SYCAMORE *(Platanus)*

SOIL AND PLANTING

If there's magic in great gardens, it's in the soil. That's why seasoned gardeners are so quick to advise you to feed the soil, not the plant, or to spend $10 on the soil, $5 on the plant. Good soil stimulates plant growth; bad soil retards it. The perfect soil is loam: a balanced combination of sand, silt, clay, organic matter, moisture, and air. It must drain well, and—for azaleas, rhododendrons, and camellias—it should be on the acid side of the pH scale. Few gardens have this legendary medium, but it's possible to make whatever soil you have more friendly to your plants. The first step is to take stock of what you've got.

A soil test will let you know what your soil is lacking.

START WITH A SOIL TEST

How good or bad is your garden soil for your plants? You can find out with scientific precision by paying for a soil test. Just call your county cooperative extension office and ask for the name of a good soil test lab. Some universities will do the job for you, but in most states the work is done at a commercial lab.

The procedure is simple: you collect a quart of soil—1 cup from each of four locations around your garden—and mix it all together in a resealable plastic freezer bag. Don't take samples from the surface; get them from 3 to 4 inches down. You want to learn about the soil that the roots will be growing in.

If your garden has more than one type of soil—clay bottomland below a fast-draining slope, for example—order separate tests for each of the soil types that will be home for your azaleas, rhododendrons, and camellias.

Before you mail the sample off, call the lab that will be doing the work and explain that you want a basic homeowner's soil profile—something that will help you grow better azaleas, rhododendrons, and camellias. Find out the charges ($40 to $50 is common) and exactly what you'll get for your money. At minimum, you'll need information about your soil's texture, pH (relative acidity or alkalinity), organic content, and nutrients.

Some labs offer a report written in simple English that describes what's wrong with your soil and how much fertilizer or amendment to apply to fix it. Unless you're a soil scientist, that's the kind of information you need, even if it costs a few dollars extra.

LEARNING ABOUT SOIL ON YOUR OWN

For at least a few thousand years, gardeners have learned about the soil they cultivate by doing some simple tests of their own. These informal tests aren't perfect—they won't tell you if you have too little nitrogen or too much calcium in the soil, for example—but they can help you find and correct problems before they trouble your plants. (For more information on tackling soil problems, see "Solutions for Problem Soils" on page 83.)

TEXTURE. Good soil contains a mixture of mineral earth and organic matter. The mineral component is usually some combination of sand, silt, and clay, and perhaps a few rocks (see "Soil Texture and Structure" on the opposite page). To see how your soil stacks up, pick up a handful of moist soil, form it into a ball, and drop it. If it falls completely apart when it hits the ground, it's sandy. If the lump feels like modeling clay and holds together after it hits the ground, it's clay. And if it breaks into a few crumbly chunks, it's loam.

Because sandy soil is open and porous, it doesn't hold nutrients or water well. As the water flushes through, it dissolves nutrients and carries them down below the reach of plant roots. But sandy soil does contain plenty of air space (oxygen is essential to roots), warms up quickly in spring, and is easy for roots to penetrate.

Clay is the opposite: This heavy soil's tiny particles are surrounded by minuscule air spaces that are slow to take in water and slow to let it go. Clay holds nutrients well, drains poorly, stays cold longer into spring, and is harder for roots to penetrate. It's also miserable to dig.

Loam contains at least two of the three mineral particle sizes (clay, silt, and sand), plus organic matter, and is named for the predominant particle size: clay loam, silty loam, or sandy loam. From a plant's perspective, the best loam is on the sandy (light) side.

Generally, the organic matter should make up 4 to 5 percent of the soil by weight, or 25 percent by volume, but for azaleas, rhododendrons, and camellias the organic content can be considerably higher (30 to 50 percent by volume). Organic content is harder to measure, but you can get a feel for it just by handling the soil and watching how it behaves. Organic matter gives soil an open, slightly spongy texture that drains well, yet retains both air and moisture. It is easy for fibrous roots to penetrate, doesn't compact as easily as mineral subsoil, and supports lots of biological activity. Vague as all this might seem, you needn't worry: by adding organic matter, you can improve almost any soil, and there's little danger of adding too much.

SOIL pH. Soil is acid (sour), neutral, or alkaline (sweet). The pH scale, which runs from 0 (acid) to 14 (alkaline), tells just how sour or sweet the soil is; 7 is neutral. Most rhododendrons grow best at a pH of 4.5 to 5.5, while most camellias like to be in the 5.5 to 6.5 range. You can test the pH of your garden soil with a pH meter or a soil test kit. Both are available from mail-order garden supply companies.

DRAINAGE. If you've lived with your garden for long, you probably have a pretty good idea of how well it drains. Still, it's helpful to run a simple test. Dig an 18-inch-deep hole and fill it with water during dry weather. Let it drain, then fill it again. If the hole doesn't drain within 2 hours of this second filling, you have drainage problems.

SUCCESSFUL PLANTING TECHNIQUES

Most azaleas, rhododendrons, and camellias are sold either in containers full of light-weight soil mix, or balled and burlapped in heavy soil. Because the roots are fibrous and have a hard time letting go of the organic matter in which they grow, these plants are almost never sold bare root.

Nursery-grown plants usually come in plastic or papier-mâché containers that you slide off for planting. When a plant has been in the same container for too long, its roots can kink or circle around the inside of the pot. Both conditions are potentially fatal but easily corrected. Before you plant, string out the roots with your fingers as you rough up the root ball (the roots and soil clinging to them). If the encircling roots are so thick that they form a mat, you should return the plant and get another. If that isn't an option, cut through the surface layer of roots with a sharp knife and pull the matted part off, stringing out the roots that are still attached. Now you're ready to plant.

Balled-and-burlapped plants are usually field grown, then dug and wrapped in something that looks like burlap. In simpler times, it always was burlap, which you didn't have to remove before planting. You just untied the top and planted the root ball and burlap together. You had to be sure to bury the upper flaps of the burlap completely, because if they poked out above the ground, they could wick moisture up out of the root

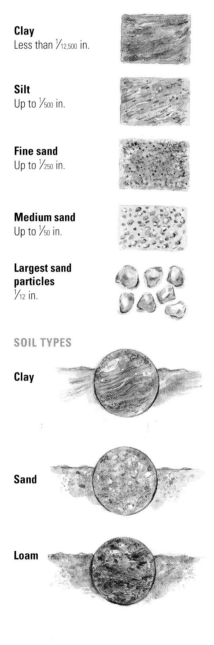

SOIL TEXTURE AND STRUCTURE

The size of mineral particles is what determines a soil's texture and designates its type: clay, sandy, or loam. Clay particles are the smallest mineral component of a soil, sand particles are the largest, and silt represents the intermediate size. A combination of three particle sizes is the basis for loam, the ideal gardening soil.

SOIL PARTICLES

Clay
Less than $1/12,500$ in.

Silt
Up to $1/500$ in.

Fine sand
Up to $1/250$ in.

Medium sand
Up to $1/50$ in.

Largest sand particles
$1/12$ in.

SOIL TYPES

Clay

Sand

Loam

STAKING A SHRUB

For plants that are top-heavy, drive two stakes into the ground about a foot on either side of the plant, perpendicular to wind direction. Loop a soft tie around one stake and then around the plant's trunk and back. Repeat with the other stake. The plant should be able to move in the wind, but not topple.

zone. But if you did everything right, the burlap would rot over time, and the plant's roots would grow normally out into the surrounding soil.

These days, burlap is not always what it seems. If it's a cheap synthetic look-alike (usually polypropylene), it will never rot once the plant is in the ground. If you suspect that the root ball is wrapped in anything except real burlap, remove it completely.

PLANTING BASICS

Planting rules for azaleas, rhododendrons, and camellias are the same. If your garden soil is reasonably good, dig a planting hole almost as deep as the root ball and three times as wide. Set the plant in the center of the hole and check it: the crown (the top of the root ball) should be about an inch above the level of the surrounding garden soil. If you plant too deeply, the plant may die—from crown rot, smothering, or a combination.

Gently spread the plant's roots out toward the hole's edges and backfill with the soil you took out, firming it up as you go. You don't need to amend the backfill (see "The Debate about Amending the Backfill" on page 84). Once the plant is in the ground, build a 4-inch-tall watering basin around it, just outside the planting hole. Fill it with water, then rock the plant slightly from side to side and firm up the native soil around the roots with your hands. You'll see bubbles coming up through the water as the plant settles in.

The first two or three times you water after the plant is in place, dig your finger into the top inch of the root ball an hour after watering to make sure it got a good drenching. If the root ball is dry, water again, even if the surrounding soil is wet.

Keep the watering basin in place during dry weather, but knock out one side of it in rainy weather. Unless the soil has outstanding drainage, too much concentrated watering will compromise the root ball.

Sometimes a plant with a small root ball and a large top can have trouble standing against the wind. If it needs support, drive two stakes into the ground, each about a foot out from either side of the plant. Their axis should be perpendicular to the direction of the wind. Then tie a ribbon of old sheet low on one stake, loop it around the plant's trunk, and bring it back to the same stake and tie it off. Do the same thing from the opposite stake. When the wind blows, the plant should move with it but not blow over (movement helps strengthen the roots). When the plant's roots are well anchored, remove the stakes.

HOW TO PLANT

Dig a hole almost as deep as the rootball and three times as wide. Build a firm mound in the center to hold root ball.

Place plant on a mound so the crown is about 1 inch above the surrounding garden soil. Gently spread roots out.

Backfill the hole with soil, firming it as you go.

Build a 4-inch-tall watering basin around the plant, just outside the planting hole. Fill with water, then rock the plant and firm up the soil.

SOLUTIONS FOR PROBLEM SOILS

There are two ways to tackle soil problems: plant by plant or bed by bed. It usually makes most sense to improve soil on a plant-by-plant basis, especially in established gardens. However, if you're facing severe problems that extend through much of the garden—if you've just moved into a new house on a lot that's been stripped to subsoil by a bulldozer, for example—you might as well rebuild all the garden soil at once.

Regardless of the scale of your soil problems, there are solutions. As you consider them, remember that when problems are interlinked, solutions may be common as well: you might be able to solve soil texture and drainage problems just by tilling in compost.

Finally, use common sense. Most soil problems have practical solutions—most, but not all. Sometimes the best way to defeat bad soil is simply to switch to planting in containers or raised beds. As a comic-strip character once said, "There's no problem so big that you can't run away from it."

SOIL TEXTURE AND STRUCTURE

Whether your soil is too heavy or too light, the solution is the same: till in organic matter. It helps sandy soil hold nutrients and water better, and helps open up the small particles in clay for better aeration and drainage.

Good choices for organic matter include compost (homemade or mushroom), leaf mold, rotted manure, ground bark, and peat moss. Aged sawdust also works, but some eastern gardeners link pine sawdust with rhododendron wilt. In the Northwest, sawdust is available composted with sewage sludge, and has proved to be a good soil amendment.

To amend any amount of ground, spread 3 to 4 inches of organic matter over it, then till or dig it in. Some tillers turn only the top 8 inches of soil, and that's okay, but amending the top 12 inches of soil will be better for your plants.

If you have the time, you can also grow a cover crop on the land you want to plant, and till it in before it goes to seed. Mail-order seed companies and local garden supply stores usually sell seeds for a variety of cover crops.

SOIL pH

If you should need to raise pH (very unlikely for azaleas and rhododendrons), add dolomitic lime to the soil. To lower it, apply ferrous sulfate (but not aluminum sulfate,

which can build up to levels harmful for azaleas and rhododendrons).

Over time, soil tends to revert to the pH it had before it was amended. You can use acid fertilizer to help keep the soil pH down. It's best to rely on lime to keep soil from becoming too acid.

Planting in clay soil requires some planning, but the results are worthwhile.

DRAINAGE

It's critical that you learn why your soil is wet before you try to drain it. Some problems (such as water running downhill into your garden) show up best during a storm, while others (such as subsurface hardpan) are easier to detect when the soil is dry enough to dig.

If a subsurface layer of hardpan is preventing water from draining deep into the subsoil, you may be able to dig through the impervious layer and open up a chimney (a dry well) into the more pervious soil below it.

If your land stays wet because water is draining onto it from higher ground, you may be able to reroute the drainage around your garden.

If you have a high water table, you may be able to lower it by ditching the edges of the garden and installing land drains through it. If you have to do this, get a landscape architect involved.

If the soil is simply too heavy, you can improve matters by tilling a 3- to 4-inch layer of organic matter deeply into the topsoil. That won't solve the problem in extreme cases, however, since the clay subsoil will still stop water from draining out of the top layer of amended soil.

The trunks of young plants may also be at risk from sunscald. This damage, which shows up as split, checked bark, is usually caused by low winter sun burning the south or east sides of unshaded trunks, especially after freezing nights.

To protect young plants, coat exposed parts of their trunks with white latex paint or wrap them loosely in white fabric. As the plant matures, the bark will thicken up and the leaf canopy will spread enough that sunscald won't pose a threat.

PLANTING IN PROBLEM SOILS

Regardless of whether you plant from containers or balled-and-burlapped stock, chances are the soil around the roots won't match the soil in your garden. If the difference between the two types of soil is great, you could run into a couple of different kinds of problems.

PLANTING IN HEAVY SOIL. There's trouble afoot when your garden soil is clay and your shrub comes rooted in lightweight potting mix. Planting in clay is like planting in a washtub: because the water you pour onto your plant is unable to percolate easily into the substrate below, it pools in the loose organic matter around the roots. Unable to survive without oxygen, the roots finally drown, and the plant wilts and dies of thirst.

You can solve this problem by planting with at least half the root ball above grade. If the plant's 3-gallon container is 10 inches deep and 10 inches wide, for example, dig a hole that's as deep as the container and three times as wide. Amend the backfill by digging in one shovelful of organic matter for every three shovelfuls of native soil and fill in all but the top 4 inches of the planting hole. Firm it up and set the root ball on top of it, then mound the rest of the backfill around it. Build a watering basin around the mound, mulch, and water.

Such mound planting allows the roots to breathe well enough to keep the plant healthy, but it also allows the plant to dry out more quickly in hot, clear weather. Be sure to check soil moisture regularly.

PLANTING IN LIGHT SOIL. If a shrub is grown in heavy soil, balled and burlapped for sale, then planted in lighter garden soil, you have what soil scientists call an interface problem. The root ball's heavier soil tends to shed, or resist, water, forcing it to run off into the more porous surrounding soil. That water won't soak into the root ball until the surrounding soil is completely drenched.

Here's what to do: Start by taking the fabric off the root ball, no matter what it's made of. Gently fork some of the dirt away from the roots on the sides of the root ball, then plant. If you make sure the roots you've just freed up make good contact with the native soil outside the root ball, they'll grow into it more readily.

You can also improve matters by digging organic matter into the soil in the planting hole, making a watering basin around the root ball, and keeping the plant from drying out completely until it's well established.

TRANSPLANTING BASICS

Because of their vigorous, fibrous root systems, azaleas, rhododendrons, and camellias are relatively easy to transplant. Although you can move plants in mild weather anytime of year, it's best to do it when they're not actively growing. If you live in a cold-winter climate—where the ground may freeze and snow falls every winter—do your transplanting in early spring. If you garden in a mild-winter southern or West Coast climate, transplant in autumn.

Water deeply 2 or 3 days before you dig your plant so that it will be in the best possible shape when you move it. Transplanting in the evening will be easiest on the plant, since it will have all night to take up water before it has to face the heat of the day.

The guiding principle is to take as much of the root ball as you can manage. Ideally, the diameter should be at least half the shrub's height. For a 4-foot plant, the rootball might be 24 to 30 inches wide and 14 inches deep. For a taller plant, you might be forced to take much less—perhaps a third of the plant's height—just because you can't physically lift and move more than that.

After you've calculated how much root ball you can handle, you'll need to dig around the plant to get at the root ball. Cut around the outside edge of the root ball with vertical stabs of a spade. Each cut should be about 11 inches deep—the full depth of the spade blade. Now cut around the plant again, this time about 8 inches outside the original circle, but with the spade's blade angled in toward the bottom of the root ball. Remove the soil.

Most of the rest of the job involves undercutting the root ball. Work all the way around it, with the spade's blade angled down. You'll wind up with a root ball that's flat on top and rather dome-shaped underneath. As you work, you'll have to chop through some sizeable roots by main force. If you can't do it with the shovel blade, cut the roots with loppers.

Keep working until you've cut completely through the underside of the root ball. You'll have to pull the plant over to make the last cuts. Be careful when you do it: some varieties of rhododendrons, of which 'President Roosevelt' is the most famous, are prone to breaking off at the crown if you pull too hard on the trunk.

Once the plant is undercut, rock or pry it over to one side of the hole and slip the rolled end of a half-rolled tarpaulin or piece of burlap as far under it as possible. Then rock the plant back to the opposite side and unroll that end of the tarp. Now you have the shrub on a hammock-like sling.

Keeping the root ball intact, gardeners use an aluminum skid to slide this large rhododendron into its new location.

If the plant is light enough, if you're not moving it far, and if you have enough help, you can lift it out on the sling and carry it to its new location. If it is too heavy or has to be moved some distance, tie the fabric around the root ball, rock the plant far over onto one side of the hole, and slip stout boards underneath it. Then slide it up into a wheelbarrow or truck or onto a tractor trailer and move it to its new location. Replant and water the shrub right away.

There's some debate over whether to top-prune transplants after you move them. Those in favor of top pruning say that after transplant, leaves lose more moisture than the chopped-off root system can easily replace, putting the whole plant at risk. By thinning the top by a third to half, you decrease the number of leaves that transpire (give off) moisture.

On the other side are specialists who have successfully transplanted 15-foot unpruned camellias with few problems. They oppose top pruning because it tends to force new vegetative growth just when the plant needs all its energy to replace lost roots. To keep unpruned transplants from drying out, they water frequently by overhead sprinklers until roots regenerate and start to function normally.

You can do two other things to reduce water loss to new transplants: remove the flower buds, since they demand lots of water to unfurl into beautiful bloom; and put 3 to 4 inches of mulch over the root zone as soon as you've completed the transplant.

Watering and Mulching

The key to success when watering and mulching azaleas, rhododendrons, and camellias is remembering where so many of these plants came from: places with wet summers and cool, rather dry winters. These are plants that like moisture—both in the soil and in the atmosphere—during the growing season. Rain or irrigation gives it to them, and mulch helps keep it from evaporating before the roots can use it. Although the three plant groups have slightly different water and mulch needs, the same general principles apply to all of them. Pay special attention to container-grown plants: they become saturated or parched more easily than plants growing in the ground.

Overhead watering of these rhododendrons planted under shade trees approximates their native rain forest conditions.

WATERING GUIDELINES

Where you live has much to do with how you water. In the United States, the 100th meridian—which runs north to south from North Dakota through Texas—is the dividing line between wet and dry parts of the country. East of the 100th meridian, gardeners usually get substantial summer rain—often enough to water all but newly planted azaleas, rhododendrons, and camellias. West of it, gardeners count on dry summers in most places, even in the Pacific Northwest; if they don't water, their plants—especially rhododendrons—will definitely suffer and perhaps die.

Each plant's tenure in your garden also has something to do with its need for water. Older, established plants need less. New transplants have relatively smaller, shallower root systems, which dry out faster, so they need more. Also, young plants put on growth much faster than older ones, and they need extra water to support it.

Soil and exposure make a difference, too. Full sun and any amount of wind cause plants to use up water faster, and sandy soils dry out faster than heavy soils. Finally, raised beds and containers drain quickly, so plants growing in them need to be watered more often.

HOW AND WHEN TO WATER

Azaleas, rhododendrons, and camellias all need the most water during their active, spring-through-summer growing season, and they all can tolerate some drought when they're not in active growth. Watering basins will direct water to the roots when they need it, but break out a side during periods of extended rain (see "Planting Basics" on page 82).

During dry times, water deeply and infrequently to encourage roots to reach down deep into the soil for moisture. If you water often and shallowly, roots will concentrate near the soil surface, where they're more vulnerable to drying out and dying in hot, dry weather. A good rule of thumb is to wait until the top 1 to 2 inches of soil under the mulch is dry before you water—more shallow for newly planted shrubs, deeper for well-established shrubs.

In some areas, especially parts of California, the water contains too much salt. That salt accumulates around the roots, causing leaf margins to burn and plants to become chlorotic. To flush salt down below root level, you have to flush the root zone every 6 months or so. It takes three times as much water as the soil can hold to effectively flush the soil: water to saturation once, let it drain through, then flood it to saturation twice more. Because this is an inexact science, most gardeners just let the hose run slowly

Mulches keep the soil cool and moist in summer and protect plants in winter.

into the watering basin for 2 or 3 hours and call it good. It's easier with plants in containers, since the medium they're in is usually so porous.

In a perfect world, you'd irrigate by hose-watering the basins around each plant during flowering season. That would keep the water from spotting the flowers and eliminate water wasted on spaces between the plants.

But in the real world, most gardeners—especially those with lots of plants—usually water with impact sprinklers on risers that put them above the shrubs. Overhead watering is especially effective in dry-summer areas, since it helps keep humidity up and washes dust off the leaves, though it may cause some spotting. The best time to water this way is in early morning, when there's minimal water loss to evaporation; if you irrigate at night, standing water on leaves and flowers can invite disease.

AZALEAS. These plants—especially deciduous azaleas—can survive with considerably less water than rhododendrons, but don't press your luck: they grow better with even moisture at the roots. Gradually cut back watering in early fall to help harden them off for winter. Drooping leaves mean the plant is too dry at any season—but it's best not to let the plant get that dry.

RHODODENDRONS. Like azalea leaves, rhododendron leaves become dull and droopy when they don't have enough water. Sometimes very hot weather can cause the same thing to happen, but when that's the case, leaves perk up in the cool of the evening. If there's any doubt, water. Late-flowering rhododendrons especially suffer from summer drought because they're still expanding new leaves long after the earlier-flowering varieties have finished. That growing process takes extra water; if it isn't available, new growth may be stunted. Gradually cut back watering in early fall to help harden off plants for winter.

BUILDING A WATERING BASIN

During dry weather, a watering basin that extends to the drip line will direct water to the plant's roots. Break out a side during rainy weather.

CAMELLIAS. When they're out of flower, these plants—as well as rhododendrons and azaleas—benefit from overhead watering, which can rinse some mites and aphids off the leaves and give predatory insects a clearer shot at the pests that remain.

Beware of underwatering. Unlike rhododendrons, camellias don't wilt until they're near death, and they don't recover easily. Also, if you let plants dry out for too long after flower buds have formed, the buds may drop off.

MULCHING GUIDELINES

Whatever your soil or circumstances, mulch does several jobs: It helps keep the soil it covers cool and moist in summer, it discourages weeds, and it insulates tender roots against freezing in winter. As the mulch breaks down, it adds organic matter to the soil, acidifies it, and feeds the roots below.

APPLYING MULCH EFFECTIVELY

Apply mulch when you plant, always over damp soil, then renew it by adding fresh mulch every autumn. There's nothing magic about autumn—it's just an easy time to remember to do it, since nature supplies lots of fallen leaves for mulching then.

You can mulch with just about any organic material. Oak leaves and conifer needles are great, as are ground bark, straw, pine straw, and compost (use the rough material that remains after you sift your compost). Avoid materials that will mat, such as wet cut grass, or pack, like fine sawdust. (Coarse sawdust is fine, and may boost growth of rhododendrons; however, pine sawdust has been linked to rhododendron wilt on the East Coast.)

AZALEAS AND RHODODENDRONS. Scale the mulch to the plant. Low-growing azaleas might do with just 1 or 2 inches, while a very large rhododendron might take 4 to 6 inches of loose mulch. Don't allow azalea flowers with petal blight (see page 110) to become part of the mulch; the blight can overwinter there.

CAMELLIAS. Camellias don't demand as thick a mulch as rhododendrons; 2 to 4 inches is fine. Don't allow camellia flowers to become part of the mulch, since many of the flowers will probably carry camellia petal blight, which can reproduce in the mulch under the plant. Pick flowers off when they show signs of blight (see page 111), and send them out with the trash.

FERTILIZING

When nurseries grow azaleas, rhododendrons, and camellias in containers, they often use a soilless planting medium that contains no nutrients of its own. The nursery people have to add all the fertilizer the plants need to grow, and they tend to do it generously so that the plants reach salable size quickly.

Because of this practice, when you transplant an azalea, rhododendron, or camellia, it quickly exhausts whatever nutrients remain in its root zone and has to reach out into surrounding soil to get the nutrients it needs. By fertilizing at the edges of the root zone, you help encourage root spread into native soil.

Always water before you apply dry fertilizer. If plants are wilted, water and wait for them to perk up before you feed. When you do sprinkle it on, there are several things you can do to make it stay put, and not wash away: scratch it into the soil; pull the mulch back, sprinkle the fertilizer, then pull the mulch back over it; or mix it well into the mulch.

TYPES OF FERTILIZERS

Plants need three major nutrients—nitrogen (N), phosphorus (P_2O_5), and potassium (K_2O)—and several minor nutrients. The proportions of the major nutrients are listed in order (in the short form "N-P-K") on the label under "Guaranteed analysis." For example, a 10-8-6 fertilizer contains 10 percent nitrogen, 8 percent phosphorus, and 6 percent potassium. Because it contains all three major nutrients, it's called a complete fertilizer. Simple fertilizers include only one major nutrient, while incomplete fertilizers contain two.

Nitrogen speeds vegetative growth and gives leaves a rich green color. Phosphorus promotes root activity and the maturing of plant tissues, necessary for flower production. Potassium encourages the manufacture of sugars and starches within the plant.

Plants need nitrogen most during the first half of the growth period. Outdoors, a growth period is triggered by the proper combination of temperature, moisture, and day length: for most plants this occurs in spring, when the weather is warming and moisture is plentiful.

At other times of the year when the weather is as warm as or warmer than it is in early spring and if moisture is available, an application of nitrogen will trigger more new growth. (Don't use too much nitrogen where water is short; more growth, after all, demands more water.) In a greenhouse or frost-free climate, this capability can be an advantage: you can push plants to grow to a larger size in less time. But for most rhododendron growers, new growth late in the season is a potential problem rather than a blessing. Summer temperatures increase transpiration rates, and young growth will wilt easily unless watering is carefully managed. Late growth has less time than spring growth to mature properly before the onset of cool autumn weather; and where frosts or freezing winters are common, young growth is likely to be damaged or killed. For these reasons, don't apply high-nitrogen fertilizer after midsummer if you garden in a climate that gets hard freezes in winter.

At nurseries and garden centers, you'll find general purpose fertilizers, as well as ones labeled specifically for azaleas, rhododendrons, and camellias. The specialty fertilizers are formulated to acidify the soil, and usually derive their nitrogen from ammonium sulfate. That's useful if your soil is not naturally acid (see page 81 for a discussion of pH), but if your soil is already in the right range for azaleas, rhododendrons, and camellias, there's little advantage to using an acid fertilizer. In such cases, general purpose fertilizers usually cost less and work as well, unless they contain calcium nitrate, which can increase the soil pH to undesirable levels.

Commercial fertilizers come in either granular or liquid form. Granular fertilizers are usually cheaper, and are designed to be scattered over the root zone two or three times each year—less for slow-release formulations. To encourage roots to grow out into native garden soil, sprinkle the fertilizer over the mulch in a band that straddles the edge of the drip line (the outside edge of the plant); apply a foot-wide band around small plants, a 2- to 3-foot band around large plants. To keep the fertilizer around the roots, where it belongs, pull back the mulch and sprinkle the fertilizer underneath, scratch it into the soil over the roots, or at least mix it into the mulch as well as you can; then water it in.

Liquid fertilizer usually comes as soluble concentrate that you dissolve in water for application. It can be used in one of two ways: as a spray applied to the plants' leaves (called foliar feeding), or as a drench poured over the roots. Because liquid fertil-

Forms of fertilizer include, clockwise from left, liquid-soluble crystals (mounded and dissolved in water), dry granules, organic fish meal, and timed-release pellets.

izer is much less concentrated than granular, and because it flushes through the soil faster, you have to apply it more frequently—as often as every 3 weeks during the growing season. Do foliar feeding in the cool of the morning, when leaves are better able to absorb it. Because liquid fertilizer washes into the root zone quickly and can be absorbed directly by leaves, it gets nutrients into the plant almost immediately. It's also clean to handle (granular fertilizers can be dusty, make you sneeze, and get all over your hands and clothes) and convenient (you can apply it with a hose-end sprayer).

FEEDING SCHEDULES

The following feeding schedules are based on using a granular fertilizer. At each feeding time, it takes about a handful of fertilizer per mature plant to do the job, but don't put it on any heavier than you'd put salt on your corn or sugar on your grapefruit, as a wise rhododendron specialist once advised. If you're after more precision, a good rule of thumb is to apply 1 level tablespoon per foot of plant growth (for example, give a 2-foot-tall plant 2 tablespoons of complete fertilizer). The general rule for liquid fertilizers is to apply 1 gallon for each 3 feet of the shrub's diameter, about every 3 weeks.

FEEDING AZALEAS AND RHODODENDRONS

Feeding schedules depend on the plant's age. Young plants need extra fertilizer to get established quickly, while mature plants don't usually need much at all. Here's a schedule that will give you healthy plants that bloom well and hold up to the vicissitudes of weather. In principle, it's best not to feed plants after midsummer, since fertilizer encourages plants to put on new growth that may not harden off in time to withstand fall frosts.

AT PLANTING TIME. Before planting, some azalea and rhododendron specialists dig fertilizer (such as 10-10-6 plus trace elements) into the soil. A good organic formula fortifies the planting soil with composted manure for nitrogen, rock phosphate for phosphorus, and greensand for potassium. The rock phosphate is important because phosphorus is difficult to get

SPREADING FERTILIZER

Spread granular fertilizer in a circle that straddles the edge of the plant's drip line.

into the root zone after planting (it doesn't move through the soil easily); but because rock phosphate is high in calcium, you should use only half the dose recommended on the label. (Calcium is a problem for rhododendrons and azaleas because most grow in calcium-poor soil in nature. When oversupplied with calcium, they can easily overdose on it and die.) Apply all other ingredients according to label directions.

When a newly planted azalea or rhododendron drops its lower leaves, the reason is usually because the plant had to use up the nutrient reserves it stored there. It's also a sign that it needs feeding. If this is the case, sprinkle a complete granular fertilizer like a 10-10-6 plus trace elements on top of the soil and water it in well.

IN EARLY SPRING. As buds swell (but well before bloom), apply 10-8-6 granular rhododendron fertilizer or a complete slow-release fertilizer.

AT LEAF EMERGENCE. New leaves start growing just as blooms fade. After they unfold completely, apply another light dose of 10-8-6 or complete slow-release fertilizer, especially if new leaves look pale.

IN FALL. Most plants don't usually need fall feeding, but they may benefit from topdressing with rotted manure in October. In parts of California with too much salinity in the soil or water, use compost instead of manure. If you have plants that didn't put on much growth and look like they need a boost, you can give them a dose of 5-10-10 granular fertilizer.

FEEDING CAMELLIAS

Camellias that grow in cool climates need less fertilizer than those in warmer climates with a longer growing season. *Camellia japonica* varieties tend to benefit from a little more fertilizer than other camellias, but no camellia needs much nitrogen; too much can burn or even defoliate plants.

AT PLANTING TIME. Don't fertilize until a few weeks after planting. Then pick up the following schedule.

AT LEAF EMERGENCE. As the first leaves appear, apply fish emulsion at half strength.

DURING THE GROWING SEASON. Fertilize at 6 week intervals beginning 6 weeks after leaf emergence. If your soil is not naturally acid, give each plant a handful of a blend of 5 parts cottonseed meal, 1 part blood meal, and 1 part iron chelate; or a half-strength drench with acid liquid fertilizer. If your soil is already acid, use camellia fertilizer or a general-purpose complete fertilizer applied at half strength. Don't fertilize after August 1st.

DURING THE DORMANT SEASON. Apply a half-strength bloom fertilizer such as 0-10-10, or low-nitrogen fertilizer such as 2-10-10 in November, December, and January; get a formulation that includes iron and zinc to help red-flowered camellias color up better.

Bypass hand
pruners

Anvil hand
pruners

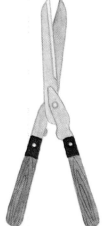

Hedge shears

Bypass loppers

Anvil loppers

PRUNING, DEADHEADING, AND DISBUDDING

In the broadest sense, anytime you remove branches, leaves, flowers, buds, or spent blossoms, you're pruning. You're taking something away from the plant so that it can direct its energies into something else, or so that it will look better. People rightly compare pruning with child-rearing: make your course corrections early, and things tend to work out well in the long run; let small problems go, and they'll become big trouble later.

PRUNING THE PLANT

The best time to prune azaleas, rhododendrons, and camellias is right after flowering, before new leaf and flower buds develop. You can prune later if it's more convenient—in fact, you can prune anytime the weather is above freezing—but unless you prune right after bloom, you'll be removing next year's flower buds as you cut out branches.

THE RIGHT TOOLS FOR THE JOB

If you can afford only two pruning tools, buy a good pair of bypass pruners and a pruning saw. They'll serve you well for most plants in your garden. Other specialized tools can fill in when you're doing great amounts of heavy pruning.

Hand pruners are either bypass pruners (also called secateurs) and anvil pruners. A full-size version of either should be able to take off a branch the diameter of your thumb without any problem. Clean cuts heal over fastest, so keep pruners sharp (good ones have replaceable blades).

Bypass pruners have a razor-sharp cutting blade that slices past a hook-shaped, sharpened lower blade. These pruners make the cleanest cut. Hold them with the cutting blade closest to the trunk to keep stub ends shorter. When you're trying to cut through large branches, don't give into the temptation to twist the shears as you make the cut or you might permanently spring (misalign) the blades and ruin the shears.

Anvil pruners have one sharp blade on top and a flat "anvil" below that the blade cuts against. These pruners don't make as clean a cut—the bottom of the cut branch might be slightly crushed by the anvil—but anvil pruners are less likely than bypass pruners to become sprung through misuse.

Loppers are like bypass or anvil pruners, but with long (20-inch) handles and oversize blades. Use them for branches thicker than your thumb.

Pruning saws can handle just about any diameter branch a rhododendron or camellia can grow. They're smaller than loppers and come with either folding or fixed blades. Look for one with a thin blade that cuts on the pull stroke. When used with a pull stroke, blades don't need to be as thick as they do for saws that push through wood—and thinner blades go through the wood more easily. Also, finer teeth make a cleaner (but slower) cut than teeth that are spaced farther apart. Many Japanese pruning saws fit the bill very well.

Pole pruners are mounted to extensions that let you get to the tops of tall shrubs. They cut with a saw, bypass blades, or anvil blades. If you're working around power lines, get one with a fiberglass or wooden extension pole so you won't be electrocuted if you accidentally bite into a power line with the cutting end.

Hedge trimmers are sometimes used to shear azaleas. Electric hedge trimmers are best for large jobs, whereas good manual hedge shears work fine for smaller jobs. Keep both away from large-leafed plants: shearing will chop or shred them into ugliness.

Orchard ladders are three-legged stepladders designed to get you in close to tall shrubs and short trees. They're extremely useful—better, some say, than pole pruners for putting you where you need to be to make close, accurate cuts in high places.

GENERAL GUIDELINES

Most azaleas, rhododendrons, and camellias do well without much pruning, but sooner or later you'll probably want to thin your plants to correct their shapes, take out damaged branches, scale plants down, or promote better penetration of air, light, and pesticides (if you need them).

A general set of pruning rules applies for almost any kind of plant, from roses to fruit trees, rhododendrons to camellias. These easy principles take the mystery out of pruning and let you accomplish the basics before you have to concern yourself with how to shape your plants. Beyond these general rules, some specifics apply to azaleas, rhododendrons, and camellias.

HOW TO PRUNE

Work from the bottom of the plant to the top, and from the inside out.

Make sure you've traced out all the tributary branches that will come off before you make each cut. You can cut, but you can't put back.

Walk all the way around the plant occasionally during the pruning process to make sure your cuts are balanced—that is, you're not taking too much or too little from any part of the shrub.

Don't make cuts flush with the trunk; instead, cut just outside the branch collar (the wrinkly bark that encircles the place where branch meets trunk). The branch collar acts as a barrier that keeps decay and disease from moving from the stub into the trunk. Or cut branches ¼ to ½ inch above a bud or side branch that points in the direction you want new growth to take.

Make pruning cuts just outside the branch collar to help protect plants from decay and disease.

If you cut a main branch back to just above a side branch, it's best to choose a side branch that's at least a third the diameter of the branch you're removing; smaller branches may not be strong enough to take over and direct growth of the trimmed branch.

Don't coat wounds with pruning paint. Wounds from pruning heal faster if they're left open to the air.

Japanese saw

Curved pruning saw (rigid)

Straight pruning saw

Bow-frame pruning saw

Curved pruning saw (folding)

Pole pruner with saw and lopper

Electric hedge trimmer

WHAT TO CUT

Prune out dead, diseased, and injured wood first.

If two branches run closely parallel, cut one out to give the other room to grow and flower.

When you find crossing branches— ones that form an ×—cut out one of them, especially if they rub against one another.

Prune out branches that grow back into the shrub instead of out toward the light.

Remove weak, spindly branches that don't do a good job of supporting their own weight or the weight of their flowers. Some varieties of azaleas, rhododendrons, and camellias tend to have many of these wiry branches; you'll never solve the problem with them completely, but you can improve matters by favoring heavier, well-supported growth with your pruning.

PRUNING SPECIFICS

Evergreen azaleas and small-leafed rhododendrons are packed with growth buds, so you can cut them just about anywhere. That's why they lend themselves to shearing and shaping—something gardeners in Japan have taken to an eye-pleasing extreme art with the Satsuki azaleas.

Deciduous azaleas sometimes produce fewer flowers as stems age. You can rejuvenate them by thinning out some of the oldest branches each year. Cut them back to the base, and the fresh growth that replaces them will bloom better. You can also freely head back or shear deciduous azaleas, and they'll regrow from their ubiquitous buds.

Large-leafed rhododendrons must be cut just above a whorl of leaves, a growth scar (where wrinkled bark shows the beginning of last season's growth), a bud, or a side branch. In most cases, new growth will break out just below your cut. Next year's

Prune camellias above a leaf, bud, or side branch.

rhododendron flowers will form on this year's new growth. Make your cuts with that in mind.

Camellias are cut above a leaf, bud, or side branch. If you cut above a leaf, choose one that points in the direction you want the new branch to grow: the shoot that emerges from the bud in the leaf axil (the joint between leaf and stem) will grow in the same direction as the leaf itself. You can thin out old plants to reinvigorate them and encourage heavier flowering.

SPECIALIZED PRUNING

In several instances, standard pruning isn't enough to achieve the shape you want. It takes something extra to turn a camellia or rhododendron into an espalier, a tree, or a hedge. Here's what to do.

ESPALIERS

We may not have many walled gardens in America, but we do have an abundance of walls and fences, each of which is reason enough to train an azalea, a rhododendron, or a camellia in two dimensions. The process, called espalier, was turned into high art by the Belgians, and it has other advantages as well: the most important may be that training a plant beneath an eave gives it overhead protection from rain.

The best candidates for espalier are camellias, whose young branches are supple and easy to train, and whose bloom keeps coming over a much longer season than either azaleas' or rhododendrons'. But people do espalier azaleas, albeit rarely, and rhododendrons as well.

Sometimes nurseries carry started sasanqua camellia espaliers, their heads fanned and pinned against latticework trellises plunged into nursery pots. But even if you can't find a prestarted espalier, you can make one using *C. sasanqua*, *C. japonica*, or *C. reticulata* varieties. Buy a plant with limber new growth whose branching pattern already tends to grow in a single plane. Then take it home and start pruning.

ESPALIER PATTERNS

Double-U

Candelabra

Belgian fence

Belgian arch

Fan

Remove any shoots that are perpendicular to the plane of growth, and loosely tie branches to a fence with plastic nursery tape or twine; or tie branches to a trellis or wire frame you've installed next to a wall. Check the tape or twine periodically to make sure it isn't starting to strangle expanding branches.

You can train a plant to grow into a fan, horizontal cordon, candelabra, or just about any other shape you can think of, though flowering tends to be best on branches that are trained horizontally. For such controlled growth, you'll need to prune every couple of months during the growing season.

With most camellias, flowers bloom on the tips of the previous spring's new growth. To guarantee an espalier's future blooms, nip out older side branches in favor of newer ones when you prune.

Before you start the training process, choose your wall carefully. A south- or west-facing wall can cook most azaleas, rhododendrons, and camellias if it gets full sun in a hot-summer climate. If it's in filtered shade during the heat of the day or if it's in a mild climate, it might be fine. By the same token, a north- or east-facing wall can be a good choice if it gets plenty of light as well as protection against cold winter winds.

HEDGES AND STANDARDS

Evergreen azaleas and smaller-leafed camellias make the best formal hedges because they take best to shearing. To get started, you'll need to do some homework. Pick a variety whose flowers you like, and find out how wide the plant is expected to grow in 10 years. Space plants at intervals equal to a third to half that width; for example, if the variety you choose is expected to grow 6 feet wide in 10 years, set plants out at 2- to 3-foot intervals and let them grow together.

As plants grow, shear them so that the widest part is at the base, the narrowest at the top. This technique helps keep the bottom part of the hedge from being shaded out.

Because larger-leafed camellias and rhododendrons are mutilated by shearing, they do better when grown as informal or semiformal hedges. It's a role they assume easily, since most garden varieties are naturally dense and shapely when they're grown in plenty of sunlight.

Plant these camellias and full-size rhododendrons at 3- to 4-foot intervals, and hand-shape them with bypass pruners—never shears. The process takes a little time, but it results in lush, natural-looking plants with whole leaves. Since both rhododendrons and camellias flower on year-old wood

Azaleas take well to training, including as bonsai.

TOP: Camellias are easily trained as espaliers, which let you show off their beauty against a wall or fence.

BOTTOM: Rhododendrons are a good choice for a large, informal hedge.

(branches that appeared the previous growing season), preserve as much of that recent growth as possible for a good flower show.

You can make standards—lollipop-shaped plants on tall, bare trunks—from camellias or evergreen azaleas. Start by training plants to a single trunk. As new growth forms at the top, prune off side branches lower down, and rub out side growth as it appears.

When the top growth is where you want it (usually 3 to 6 feet above ground level), form it into a dense ball by using hedge-pruning principles. Shear (azaleas only) or hand-prune tip growth to concentrate well-branched, dense growth in a 15- to 24-inch globe at the top of the plant.

DO-IT-YOURSELF TREES

Because so many rhododendrons and camellias grow to huge proportions in the wild, some gardeners train them as garden-scale flowering trees. Just start with a plant that has large size in its genes (that's almost any camellia, especially *C. reticulata*, and very many rhododendrons), and gradually prune off lower branches, favoring one, three, or five trunks.

As the plant grows, new sprouts may emerge from the trunk. If they do, just rub them out with your thumb. (Many kinds of rhododendrons—notably members of the Falconeri and Thomsonii series—don't usually resprout from bare trunks.)

Though your aim is to produce a traffic-stopping flowering tree, don't plan on growing it in the open, where leaves may scorch. Plant it under or to the north of taller trees that will give it protection against leaf scorch but permit enough filtered sun to pass through so it will flower well.

Training a rhododendron can produce a traffic-stopping tree.

RESTORING OVERGROWN PLANTS

When a camellia or rhododendron grows out of control, hard pruning may be the best way to restore it. Do it during mild weather in early spring.

Most healthy rhododendrons and camellias are remarkably responsive to severe pruning: chopped off a foot above ground level, many otherwise healthy old plants have quickly grown back. You may not want to try anything that radical, but don't be afraid of hard pruning either.

If you have a healthy plant that's a third taller than it should be, you can safely cut it back by half immediately after bloom. The plant will produce new growth to replace the old within a few weeks, probably give you a few flowers the following year, and be restored to its former glory within 2 years.

FATTENING UP LANKY PLANTS

Some azaleas, rhododendrons, and camellias tend to have rather open habits, which you can force to fill out by pinching and pruning. But one caution is in order: Almost any shrub can become lanky when it's grown in too much shade (which also inhibits flowering). When that's the case, move the plant or do some overhead pruning to give it more light.

PINCHING. Here's how pinching works. Right after bloom, pinch or twist out the slender terminal leaf buds (the buds at the branch tips) as they start to elongate. These terminal leaf buds produce hormones that keep nearby dormant leaf buds from sprouting, so when you remove them, hormone production stops, allowing lower buds to open and grow into leaves and branches. By removing one terminal leaf bud, you can make several buds grow farther down the stem, creating a much denser plant. (Terminal flower buds on rhododendrons don't produce bud-inhibiting hormones, which is why several leaf buds often sprout beneath rhododendron flowers.)

PRUNING. You can accomplish the same thing by cutting branches back to a point just above an annual growth scar (the place where last season's growth began). Again, the terminal bud comes out with the branch, so buds lower down are spurred into growth. To find the growth scar, look for wrinkled bark just below a leaf node or cluster of leaf scars (where old leaves fell off). The bark sometimes changes color there, and often shows bumps made by dormant buds beneath.

Pinching and pruning are especially effective when a plant is young, since that's when it needs to develop strong scaffold branches that form the framework of the plant. Don't pinch or prune branches with more than one terminal leaf bud, since multiple buds will make multiple branches—just the results you're after.

Pinching works well with rhododendrons and camellias, while pruning is more often used on azaleas. Each of these groups of plants has some additional quirks you should know about when it comes to shaping them.

AZALEAS. These plants often grow naturally in a beautiful tiered pattern. The spaces between the tiers give the plants character, so there's usually little point in trying to force them to fill in. But occasionally you'll need to head back a plant when growth is too irregular, or when broken branches leave obvious holes in the plant's canopy.

RHODODENDRONS. Rhododendrons may have one, two, or three growth spurts per year. The first is in spring, immediately after flowering; the second (if it comes) a couple of months later; and the third a couple of months after that. Growth spurts start when leaf buds start to stretch out into branches and leaves.

At the end of each growth spurt, as new leaves and branches begin to harden off, new buds form. They can be either slender leaf buds, fat flower buds, or both. Leave the flower buds alone, but pinch the leaf buds (if there's only one per branch tip) just as they begin to elongate.

CAMELLIAS. Generally, camellias don't need to be made more dense. There are some exceptions, however, including most *C. reticulata* varieties and a few lanky varieties of *C. japonica* and *C. sasanqua*. To force branching on nursery plants, try pinching; for established plants, go with pruning.

Whichever technique you use, it's best to do it immediately after flowering. Camellia varieties usually have just one growth spurt per year, but some varieties have up to three. You can pinch out leaf buds that form after any of the three spurts has hardened off.

Varieties of *C. reticulata* are the toughest cases because they often react so badly to pruning: head a branch back and it may respond by dying back farther than you'd intended—or by dying out completely. If you want to control it by pruning, head it back to a bud that is obviously starting to develop.

PRUNING FLOWERS OR BUDS

Though most pruning is designed to redirect growth, flower pruning is mostly cosmetic. You twist off buds to make those that remain produce bigger flowers, you cut fresh flowers to enjoy indoors, or you pull off dead blooms to make the plant look better (and to grow more vigorously). It's cosmetic—but it's pruning nonetheless. Do it right and the plant will prosper; do it badly and you'll wish you hadn't done it at all.

FOR THE VASE

Azaleas, rhododendrons, and camellias all make good cut flowers, but they're used differently. Here are some guidelines.

AZALEAS. Evergreen azaleas are especially beautiful plants for indoor arrangements. Florists sell them whole in pots, but home gardeners usually just nip off whole flowering branches and display them in vases. Cut anywhere along a branch; azaleas have so many growing points that they'll bud and regrow from wherever you cut.

RHODODENDRONS. Cut branches of early rhododendrons, such as the deciduous *R. mucronulatum* hybrids, and use them as you would azaleas in vases. Later evergreen rhododendron flowers can work in large arrangements with foliage. Just think large scale; individual trusses are so symmetrical that they're hard to work with alone unless you float them in bowls. Make your cuts just above leaf whorls.

CAMELLIAS. Camellias make the best single flowers, lasting 3 or 4 days in the vase. Cut them when blooms are just starting to open, taking one to three leaves along with each flower. You can set the flowers in small vases, float them in bowls of water, or use them as classic corsages. Cut just above a bud or side branch.

DEADHEADING

As flowers fade, many gardeners remove them. This practice, called deadheading, cleans up the plant and diverts energy from seed production to vegetative growth and next season's flowers. For azaleas and rhododendrons, deadheading is optional but helpful: without it, many varieties tend to go into an alternate flowering cycle, blooming heavily one year and lightly the next. For camellias, it's a must, since deadheading controls the spread of camellia petal blight, which overwinters on dead flowers.

Spent azalea and rhododendron flowers can go into the compost heap if they show no signs of disease. Camellia flowers should be buried under at least 5 inches of dirt, burned, or packed in plastic garbage bags and sent out with the trash.

BUD TYPES

Leaf buds are slender and narrower; flower buds are plumper. Pinch leaf buds just as they begin to elongate.

To make the garden look more trim, start by deadheading plants that are the most visible: those that flower by entries, walkways, windows, decks, or patios. Then, as time permits, work on those that are farther afield.

AZALEAS. Because azaleas have the most flowers, they're the toughest to deadhead. On a large, mature shrub, you might not be tall enough to reach all the faded flowers you want to remove. Most gardeners concentrate their deadheading efforts on deciduous azaleas (they usually produce far more seed than evergreen azaleas, so they benefit most from deadheading) and let the evergreen azaleas go.

To deadhead any kind of azalea, just grab the faded flowers (and the threadlike pistils and stamens) and pull them off.

REMOVING SPENT FLOWERS

To deadhead them, pick off each truss just above the leaf buds that are emerging below.

RHODODENDRONS. Flowers bloom in trusses (clusters that arise from single stems), usually at branch tips, so they're conspicuous. That's great when they're in glorious bloom, not so great when they die and turn brown.

To deadhead them, snap off each truss just above the leaf buds that are emerging below. You can easily do the job with your thumb and forefinger. You're sure to accidentally break off a few trusses too low—taking leaf buds out, too—but with practice, you'll learn to do it quickly and perfectly.

Some kinds of rhododendrons have sticky trusses, so you might want to use disposable rubber gloves when you remove the spent flower. Or use your bare hands and wash them with a hand cleaner that removes grease (available from any auto parts store).

CAMELLIAS. Flowers usually fall off by themselves—a fact noted in 15th-century Japan, where warriors stayed away from camellias for fear that their own heads might come off in battle just as easily. But if your plant has camellia petal blight (as most do after wet winters), pull flowers off before they drop, and dispose of them.

Because camellia petal blight is such a problem, and because deadheading can help reduce it, prune back plants to keep them low enough that all the flowers remain within reach.

DISBUDDING

Serious camellia growers remove some camellia buds every summer—especially when they plan to cut blooms for show—because disbudding makes the buds that remain produce larger flowers. There's no reason to disbud azaleas—after all, you buy them for sheets of bloom—or to disbud rhododendrons.

Do your camellia disbudding in late summer, after the roundish flower buds appear. (Leaf buds are slender and pointed.) Most camellia fanciers leave only one bud per branch tip, and no more than two buds per branch on shrubs. It's also good to take out buds (or adjacent branches and leaves) that are growing in tight quarters, since the congestion will distort them.

You can leave more buds on espaliered camellias—one every 3 to 4 inches—because more flowers look better on two-dimensional wall plants; just thin multiple flower buds to singles. However, if you have large and small buds growing together, leave both: the larger one will bloom early, the smaller one later. Remove buds by twisting them off, never by pulling.

If you live in a rainy climate and want a few perfect flowers for show or display indoors, leave a few downward-facing buds: they'll produce down-facing flowers that shed rain and stay in good shape longer for cutting.

GROWING IN CONTAINERS

Containers give you the freedom to grow azaleas, rhododendrons, and camellias in places where they couldn't otherwise be grown: in gardens with impossibly bad or diseased soil, on elevated decks or concrete patios, and in hostile climates. Where climate is a problem, containers allow you to stretch the limits with your plants. You can display them almost anywhere during bloom season, then whisk them off to cool shade or frost-free shelter when temperatures spike or crash.

Even camellias cooperate. Those that bloom in winter in mild climates will delay their flowering until spring where it's cold; to a point, you can winter them in a cool greenhouse or enclosed porch until temperatures moderate enough to move them outside, where they'll flower freely.

Most camellias do well as long-term container plants. But reticulatas don't take well to pruning, so it's difficult to keep them small enough for most pots.

Rhododendrons and azaleas are also fine container plants, but you have to pick and choose. Evergreen azaleas are naturals for container culture; that's why so many are sold as potted gift plants. Among deciduous azaleas, go for smaller ones like Northern Lights hybrids, which are also extremely hardy (to −40°F/−40°C). At the other end of the spectrum, tender Vireya rhododendrons seem designed for pots; many gardeners grow them as house plants. With the exception of rhododendrons that grow into large shrubs or trees, almost any of the small to medium kinds will work in a container.

THE BASICS OF CONTAINER CULTURE

Container-grown plants have flexibility as their first virtue. But they also have some rather unyielding special needs: ignore them at your peril, or meet them and succeed.

Soil temperature in containers varies more than soil temperature in the ground; the smaller the pot, the greater the variation. In a cold snap, frost comes at roots from the sides as well as the top, eventually freezing the root zone solid. And in summer, soil in the pot gets much warmer than garden soil, especially when the sun shines on it directly. Though plants do better with less fluctuation in soil temperature, pots still have an advantage: you can move them into a warmer or cooler place before extreme weather kicks in.

Moisture content also fluctuates more rapidly in containers than in the ground. Water saturates the soil quickly, but it also drains off fast, and during hot weather a container can dry out in a day. Impermeable containers slow water loss, as does a water-retentive soil mix.

Fertilizer levels tend to change quickly in containers as well. It goes hand in hand with the amount of water required. Water washes nutrients through the root zone and out of the pot—the more water you need, the more fertilizer you lose—so nutrients have to be continually replenished.

'Ward's Ruby' azalea adapts easily to container culture.

CONTAINER CHOICES

Garden centers and specialty outlets are loaded with containers in all shapes and sizes. Pot dimensions usually refer to the diameter at the top. A 16-inch pot, for example, is 16 inches from rim to rim, and can be any depth.

Wooden boxes, tubs, and half-barrels insulate well and look good, but they're heavy and aren't especially good at retaining moisture, especially if they have many joints that water can seep through. They also rot if they aren't pressure treated or painted with wood sealer. Some people staple sheet plastic inside to protect the wood from rot and to retain moisture, always leaving one or more drain holes (more for larger pots) open at the bottom.

Terra-cotta containers are heavy and beautiful, and they provide pretty good insulation against heat and cold. But they tend to dry out quickly in hot weather, and they can flake or crack in subfreezing weather if they aren't high-fired or sealed. You can prevent both problems by painting the pots, inside and out, with masonry sealer before you plant.

Cast concrete pots are fast replacing terra-cotta. They are strong, heavy, and relatively inexpensive, and come in a huge array of sizes and designs; some are near-perfect copies of Tuscan pots. They also insulate well.

Plastic containers are lightweight and inexpensive, retain moisture relatively well, and hold up well in freezing weather. They don't provide much insulation, however: on a mild sunny day, the temperature inside can easily run 15° warmer than a same-size, same-color terra-cotta pot. Black plastic pots can run 30° warmer. If you use them, lean toward light-colored containers. Plastic pots are available in a remarkably wide range of sizes: 1- and 2-foot plastic pots are common, while 3-footers and larger pots are available if you look.

Self-watering containers are becoming easier to find and better in quality. Most are plastic, and those that are double-walled insulate well. The best of them, available from interior plantscapers (businesses that supply plants for bank lobbies and covered shopping centers), are quite beautiful, large (up to 4 feet in diameter), and available in almost any finish you could wish for. They haven't been well tested with azaleas, rhododendrons, and camellias, but they have done a good job with everything from palms and figs to bamboos.

SOIL AND POT PREPARATION

The planting mix is more critical for containerized plants than for those growing in open ground. You can't use unamended garden soil in a container, since it will inevitably compact and kill the roots. Instead, either buy a high-quality commercial potting mix or blend one yourself.

A good basic mix that can be used to pot up any kind of azalea, rhododendron, or camellia combines 50 percent peat with 25 percent leaf mold and 25 percent sand or perlite. Many gardeners substitute aged ground bark or compost mixed with ground bark for the peat, since that combination gives the mix better drainage. There is, in fact, a great deal of latitude in what

'George Lindley Tabor' evergreen azalea

you can use. Different growers get good results with widely differing soil recipes. In many cases, the recipes vary according to what's available locally. Just remember to keep the organic fraction of your mix between 50 and 75 percent of the total volume.

For rhododendrons and camellias, but not most azaleas, coat the inside of the pot with copper hydroxide before you add the planting mix, or use a pre-coated container. When roots hit the sides of an uncoated container, they usually just keep growing along its surface until they've encircled the pot, and the plant becomes root-bound. But when roots touch a surface coated with copper hydroxide, they stop growing and send new roots out from

Rhododendron indicum 'Balsaminaeflorum' thrives in a hanging container.

closer to the center of the plant. Over time, the root system of the plant will become very dense.

Plants growing in treated containers can last about three times as long before being repotted: a camellia, for example, can be kept in the same pot for up to 6 years instead of 2. When you finally transplant a shrub that's been growing in a treated pot, the roots that had stopped at the copper hydroxide start growing again.

POTTING UP

Choose a container that's 2 to 4 inches wider than the plant's root ball and no more than 1½ times as deep, with a maximum depth of about 16 inches. If you're planting in conventional terra-cotta, plastic, or cast concrete, start by putting a shard of broken terra-cotta over the drainage hole so the soil you put in the pot won't just fall out the bottom. (Unless it's a self-watering pot, the container *must* have a drain hole.)

Now take the plant out of the container it came in and rough up the outside of the root ball, gently freeing up some of the root tips as you go. (If roots have encircled the pot, string them out and snip them off.) When you're done, most of the root ball will be intact, but the outer ½ inch will be sparsely bearded with hanging roots.

Scoop enough soil into the container so that when you set the plant on it, the top of the root ball will be just below the pot rim. Press the plant down into the mix until the top is about an inch below the rim, then add soil around the sides of the plant, firming it as you go, until the soil mix is even with the top of the root ball. Water it all in, and add soil as needed to level the soil surface in the pot.

FEEDING AND WATERING

Potting mix, water, and sunlight get a plant off to a good start, but they don't sustain it. That takes fertilizer—something most potting mixes don't have.

At planting time, you can supplement your potting mix with a light application of controlled-release or organic fertilizer to encourage roots to grow out into it. But eventually you'll have to do more to keep your plant healthy.

Controlled-release fertilizer is gaining currency among growers because it lasts. Within this type of fertilizer, nutrients are encapsulated in a permeable bead made of a substance such as resin or sulfur; when you water, the nutrients are slowly dissolved out of the capsule and into the surrounding soil. Many organic fertilizers also release their nutrients slowly and effectively. You can buy formulations that release fertilizer over any period from 3 months to a year. With most of these products, the fertilizer is released in the presence of warmth and water, so plants get the most nutrients during warm weather, when their growth is strongest.

CALCULATING VOLUME

To leach salt and alkaline from soil you need to run water through the pot at a ratio of 3 gallons water to 1 gallon soil. While the volume of individual pots depends on their shapes, it's possible get an average estimate by measuring the pot diameter. As a general rule, pot sizes to volume are as follows:

POT DIAMETER (AT RIM)	VOLUME
6 inches	1 gallon
8 inches	2 gallons
10 inches	3 gallons
11 inches	4 gallons
12 inches	5 gallons
15 inches	10 gallons
20 inches	25 gallons

So, for example, to leach a 6-inch pot, which contains 1 gallon of soil, you would need to run 3 gallons of water through it (number of gallons multiplied by 3). For an 8-inch pot, which contains 2 gallons of soil, you'd need 6 gallons of water.

With training and the proper care, even small standards can be grown in containers.

Low-growing species, such as this azalea, are effective container plants.

Camellia japonica can be maintained in a 16-inch pot almost indefinitely.

Growers who want more control tend to use either liquid fertilizer, cottonseed meal, or azalea, rhododendron, and camellia fertilizer applied monthly at half strength from just after flowering through midsummer.

Overwatering and underwatering are the two great killers of containerized plants. That's why the soil mix is so important: if it drains well but not completely—that is, if the organic part of the mix hangs onto some moisture even after most of the water has drained through—it buffers the plant against watering extremes.

Even with a good soil mix, you should check containerized plants daily in warm weather and every couple of days in cool weather. Some gardeners call it the "dirty digit test": just dig your finger an inch into the planting mix and feel it. If it's dry, water. If it's moist, leave it alone. Don't judge by the soil surface: it can be dry when there's plenty of moisture an inch down.

An hour after you water, recheck the soil over the root zone to make sure it got a good soaking. This is doubly important the first season after planting, especially if the soil around the root ball is a different type than the potting soil. In some cases, water can run through the loose outer soil without ever soaking the root ball. When that happens, submerge the whole pot in a larger bucket full of water and let it soak for a half-hour or so. That will wet the root ball, and make it easier to water the next time if it hasn't gone bone dry in the interim.

If you live in a place where the water is alkaline or salty, or if your plants are growing in self-watering containers, you'll have to flush the soil occasionally to leach out salt buildup from water and fertilizer, and chemical buildup from alkaline water. Flush plants growing in self-watering pots every six months, and plants being irrigated with alkaline or salty water every month. To do so, calculate the volume of soil in the pot, then run three times that much water through it (see the chart "Calculating Volume" on page 99).

REPOTTING AND ROOT PRUNING

Plants can usually remain in a container for two to four years—less for younger plants and those raised where the growing season is extra long, more for mature plants and those raised where the growing season is short. After that, roots start to encircle the inside of the pot unless you've coated it with copper hydroxide (see "Soil and Pot Preparation" on page 98). Even in treated pots, the day will come when you'll either have to transplant into a larger pot or do some root pruning.

The best time to repot is whenever you'd normally plant in your region: fall in mild-winter climates, early spring where winters are colder. If you're transplanting a young, vigorously growing shrub, choose a container that's 2 to 4 inches wider than the root ball.

If you're trying to maintain a mature shrub in one container indefinitely, root prune and repot it every few years. Do that by sliding the plant out of its pot and carefully working the soil off the outer 2 to 3 inches of roots. Cut the exposed roots back by at least half, and replant in fresh potting soil in the original container.

Camellias can be maintained in a 16-inch pot almost indefinitely. Smaller azaleas and rhododendrons can take much smaller pots, down to 10 inches, but a medium-size plant may need something as large as a half-barrel.

Smaller azaleas can remain in small pots to decorate patios and decks.

RAISED BEDS

Most often, bad soil or bad drainage drives gardeners to plant in raised beds—but those aren't the only good reasons for elevating your plants. Raised beds get low plants up where you can see them and put fragrant plants closer to nose level. They also help redefine your landscape, outlining patio and living areas, screening off things you don't want to see (like the compost pile), and subtly directing the flow of garden traffic.

In almost every case, a whole raised bed full of plants is better than a single shrub planted in a small mound. It simply works better: a single mound sheds water and dries out too quickly in hot weather; it also freezes too deeply in cold weather, since frost comes at the plant's roots from the sides as well as at the top. If you want a raised habitat for a single plant, put it in a pot.

BUILDING MATERIALS

The best raised beds are large, well-built parts of the hardscape. They're usually—but not always—straight sided and flat topped, since that shape catches water and delivers it to the root zone more efficiently than slope-sided berms.

The most common woods used for making raised beds are creosote-impregnated railroad ties and pressure-treated lumber, both of which do a good job resisting rot. Be careful when you handle either: Creosote is a contact carcinogen, but only repeated contact over a very long time—years, usually—causes problems. Lumber that has been pressure-treated has been injected with potentially toxic chemicals, commonly an arsenic derivative; avoid getting slivers and breathing sawdust or (especially) smoke from this type of wood.

If you opt to use regular lumber, you can treat it with wood preservative or line the wood inside the bed with sheet plastic. Don't line the bottom; the bed must drain.

Brick and stone are also outstanding materials for raised beds. In direct sun, both materials absorb and hold heat, which is an advantage in cool climates.

Beds should be at least 16 inches deep for plants that will be small at maturity, at least 2 to 3 feet deep for larger plants.

PLANTING IN A RAISED BED

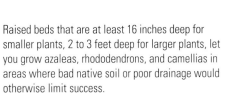

Raised beds that are at least 16 inches deep for smaller plants, 2 to 3 feet deep for larger plants, let you grow azaleas, rhododendrons, and camellias in areas where bad native soil or poor drainage would otherwise limit success.

It's true that most feeder roots are within a foot of the soil surface, but it's also true that anchoring roots can go much deeper, so you'll want to give them space.

PERFECT SOIL FOR PERFECT PLANTS

When you buy soil for raised beds that will hold azaleas, rhododendrons, or camellias, get an acid mix with high organic content and good drainage. Much "topsoil" is created by mixing fill dirt with sewage sludge, municipal compost, sawdust, or some other local product. These products work well, but ask a few questions before you buy. Find out about the pH (it should be 4.5 to 5.5 for rhododendrons, 5.5 to 6.5 for camellias), organic content (it should make up at least 4 percent by weight, 25 percent by volume), any nutrient content (many are essentially sterile, and need nutrients fairly quickly or plants will starve), and most important, whether the organic component is fully composted (aged). If the soil supplier can't tell you the pH and nutrient content of the soil, get it tested (see "Start with a Soil Test" on page 80).

The composted part of the soil should be black and broken down; you shouldn't be able to recognize the organic ingredients that went into it. Uncomposted organic matter ties up nitrogen in the mix as it decays, making this major nutrient unavailable to the plants you're trying grow.

After you've put the soil into your raised bed, water it thoroughly, let it settle for a couple of days, then water and let it settle again before you plant. Over time, you'll probably have to feed plants in raised beds a little more often than plants in the ground. Raised beds drain faster and thus need more water, which in turn washes nutrients out of the soil in the beds before plants can use them.

All the other principles of planting and growing azaleas, rhododendrons, and camellias still apply. Mulch plants, prune as needed, and watch for insects and diseases. All this attention seems somehow easier to give plants in raised beds, perhaps because they're up where you can work with them more easily.

WINTER PROTECTION

Snow-covered rhododendron

When gardeners talk about 20-year winters or 100-year winters, they're talking about serious cold—the worst anyone's seen in 20 or 100 years. These are the kinds of winters that wipe out tender plants, leaving gardeners resolved to grow only the toughest, most frostproof plants that money can buy. But then along comes a string of mild winters, and gardeners gradually start taking risks again until another savage winter sweeps through.

Cold damage to a rhododendron

Extreme cold isn't always what does in plants. Though every plant has its own hardiness limit, the cold that does the most damage is often the cold that comes too early, before plants are fully dormant in fall; or too late, after they break dormancy in spring. And almost as often, it's cold that comes on the heels of a warm spell: plants have a hard time with extreme temperature fluctuations that occur within a short period of time.

Frigid, dry winds also mean trouble for plants, especially when the ground around the roots is frozen. When the wind strips moisture out of the leaves, it needs to be replaced from the roots or the plant will dry out.

Mature, well-established plants tend to bear up better under extreme cold than their younger or recently transplanted siblings, and shrubs whose canopies go to ground level do better than those that have been pruned into standards or small trees. Taking these differences into account, there is much you can do to protect all your plants against extreme or unseasonable cold, rapid temperature swings, and drying winds.

GIVE AN EDGE TO EXISTING PLANTS

Plants that survive the cold usually have a growth cycle that goes like this: they break dormancy after the last killing frosts have passed; they grow strongly until just before midsummer; then they harden off early in preparation for the cold months. Timing your fertilizing and watering accordingly will help assure that your plants follow this cycle. Then give plants an extra measure of protection by mulching before the ground freezes, and be prepared to shelter the least hardy plants during the year's most hostile weather.

GROWTH CYCLES: MANAGING FERTILIZER AND WATER

To fuel vigorous new growth early in the season, adopt a feeding schedule that's weighted toward spring. Don't apply high-nitrogen fertilizer at all after the first of August, or the first of July in very cold-winter climates. That way you'll give plants most of the summer to harden off before fall frosts come.

Give plants heaviest irrigation when they need it most: while they're putting on new growth during spring and early summer. Taper off watering after August 1, ideally letting rain do all the late-season watering for you. That also helps plants harden off for fall. Then water again deeply (if the rain doesn't do it for you) just before the ground freezes.

There is some important fine print. Young plants need more water than well-established, mature plants; and first-year plants—those that were planted or transplanted during the previous year—need the most water of all. The same principle still holds, however: though you'll give young plants more water than older ones, you'll still water less in late summer than you did earlier.

You'll know how much water to give by watching the shrubs' leaves and the soil closely. Rhododendron and azalea leaves tend to become dull and wilted when the plant is stressed by lack of water. Don't worry about it if leaves show these conditions on a hot afternoon; but if the plant hasn't recovered by morning, water deeply. Camellias don't wilt and recover as readily as rhododendrons, so the best way to discern their real needs is by watching the soil: even in late summer, when it's dry an inch or two under the mulch, give plants water .

Whenever you water, remember that it's better to water deeply and infrequently than to water shallowly and often. Deep watering encourages deep rooting—and deep roots can pull up water from below the frost line when ground-freezing cold settles in.

MULCHES, WINDBREAKS, AND NATURAL SHELTERS FOR EXTREME WEATHER

Mulches are always a good idea for azaleas, rhododendrons, and camellias. And in winter they can mean the difference between life and death for your plants, since they keep the ground from freezing the lowest roots. Because ground freezes from the surface downward, for every 1 inch of mulch you place around a plant, you decrease the depth of the freeze by the same amount.

Cold air holds less moisture than warm air, so when it's really cold, it's almost always really dry. To protect shrubs from drying winter winds, build a windbreak between your plants and prevailing cold winds.

Solid fences and walls make poor wind breaks, since the wind hits them like a wave, breaks over them, and resumes blowing on the other side. These structures provide significant protection only for a distance equal to their height.

TOP: Ice-split bark on a rhododendron
BOTTOM: Snow-covered camellia blossom

Shrubs and trees do a much better job because they break up the wind, vastly diminishing its force. Their protective lee stretches behind them about eight times as far as the windbreak is high.

To give plants temporary protection from very hard freezes, you can cut conifer boughs and lay them over the plants you want to protect, but don't leave them on any longer than you must: broad-leafed evergreens photosynthesize all year long and need as much light as they can get, and the weight of the evergreens can permanently bend the branches down.

MAN-MADE SHELTERS FOR SHIVERING SHRUBS

Some gardeners make effective temporary windbreaks for individual plants by screening or surrounding them with burlap stapled to grape stakes or 2-by-2-inch posts. These shelters also do a good job keeping winter sun off trunks and flower buds. When extreme cold is predicted, temporarily suspend burlap over the plant as well, but don't let it touch the leaves or frost may damage them.

Putting a ready-made lath screen on the sunny or windy side of a plant, and over it as well if you like, will provide similar protection. These lath screens are sold at home centers across the country.

Full-scale lath houses and shade houses are just as effective in climates with hot summers as in those with cold winters. A shade house is like a lath house, but it is covered with shade cloth instead of laths. Both will moderate summer and winter temperatures and promote strong plant growth. If you make a lath house, lay the laths on the top along a north-south axis to prevent sunlight from remaining on any part of any plant for very long.

Cloth coverings help protect plants from frost damage.

A windbreak can provide needed protection from cold, dry winds.

STARTING FROM SCRATCH

If you're bringing tender plants into the garden for the first time, you can do several things to help them survive tough winters. The same principles can also help other outdoor garden plants stand up better to the cold.

SITING

Start by siting shrubs in a place that's sheltered from wind and partly shaded, especially from the morning sun; when that early sunlight suddenly warms buds that have been through a freezing night, it can kill them. If they're allowed to warm slowly as air temperature gradually increases during the day, they'll have a much better chance of coming through uninjured.

In cold-winter parts of the country, try to give tender plants a northern exposure. A north-facing slope or the north side of a building will be cooler than other parts of the landscape, and will inhibit plants from starting growth too early in spring and push them into dormancy earlier in fall. These conditions will help protect them against damage from late frosts in spring and early frosts in autumn.

In contrast, southern exposures (the south side of a wall, or a sunny south slope, for example) are real trouble in cold country: they gain so much more heat during the day that they induce plants to start growing too early in the season and keep them from going dormant until too late in fall. Such locations also have greater differences between daytime highs and nighttime low temperatures, which can themselves be fatal.

Because cold air is heavier than warm, cold air flows over a landscape much like water, running down slopes and valleys and pooling in low spots. Such low spots, especially when they're open to the night sky, unprotected by trees or buildings, usually record an area's lowest nighttime temperatures. Avoid landscaping these areas with borderline plants.

PLANT SELECTION AND TIMING

Plants vary in hardiness not only from variety to variety, but also according to age. Older, established plants can handle cold better than younger ones. Their roots go down deeper, bark is thicker, and their canopies are more dense, offering more protection to the roots and trunk below. Start out with larger plants—at least 3-footers—and plant them in spring, so they have the maximum amount of time possible to establish their roots before they're tested by a hard freeze. For a list of hardier evergreen azaleas, rhododendrons, and camellias, see pages 11, 51, and 68.

SMART PLANTING

Plants with deep roots have the best chance of surviving extreme cold because even when the ground freezes around roots close to the surface, the deeper roots will be able to get water. If you dig and amend the top 2 feet of soil with plenty of organic matter, you'll create the kind of deep root run that will vastly increase your plant's chances of surviving the coldest weather.

THE CONTAINER OPTION

You can grow almost any tender plant you want in a container if you have a bright, relatively frost-free place to put it during the cold months (see "Growing in Containers" on page 97). That may mean bringing it into a greenhouse or bright porch when the cold weather comes, or taking a note from many southern camellia growers who grow containerized camellias under large greenhouse frames, covering them with plastic during the winter flowering season and leaving them exposed (or covered with lath) in summer.

A WORD ABOUT SNOW

Snow tends to fall through leafless shrubs in winter, but it tends to accumulate fast on broad-leafed evergreen azaleas, rhododendrons, and camellias. If the snow is wet and heavy (as it usually is in mild parts of the Pacific Northwest), it can break branches. Your best defense is to go into the garden periodically as the snow falls and shake or knock it off the branches. It's fine to let it build up under the plants: snow's insulating ability can keep the ground over the roots from freezing.

Rhododendron zoelleri

VIREYAS

From Southeast Asia come the Vireya rhododendrons, also called Malesians. These tender plants are the indoor rhododendrons, providing color throughout the year and letting gardeners who aren't living in "Rhododendron Country" enjoy their beauty.

The vast Malay Archipelago isn't the last place you'd expect to find rhododendrons, but it probably wouldn't be your first guess either. Yet perhaps 300 species are growing there, some in tropical rain forests, some in high mountain meadows from Taiwan and the Malay Peninsula across Indonesia to New Guinea and northern Australia. Many of these are epiphytes, relying on rain and the nutrients brought by decaying leaves and other organic detritus.

The higher-elevation Vireyas seem to work best in cultivation. Their flowers can be astounding: one grows the biggest trumpets of any rhododendron; many others make waxy yellow, red, orange, or white flowers, some with elegant long tubes, others with wonderfully sweet fragrance. Best of all, most share a liking for light shade, plenty of water, and a frost-free environment—just what you'd want for an indoor plant.

Although in cultivation for more than a century and once prized and hybridized by English conservatory gardeners, these tender plants went out of fashion when giant glasshouses lost popularity. Now they're coming back—as indoor-outdoor plants for most of us, but as outdoor plants for gardeners in frost-free climates.

Vireyas come in all sizes, but specialty growers usually concentrate on ones in the 2- to 3-foot range. Many tend to be on the lanky side, but you can pinch them back when they're young to make them more compact and bushy. Some flower only once a year, others many times, usually from midwinter through early spring. Peak bloom season for Vireyas as a group is October through June.

HOW TO GROW THEM

Most gardeners grow Vireyas in containers, keeping them on an east-facing patio during the warm season and bringing them indoors during winter, when frost threatens and bloom is at its peak. You can grow them permanently in the ground outside if you live in Hawaii, Southern California, or along mild parts of the Gulf Coast. Vireyas have also been grown successfully along northern California's coastal fog belt, but if you try this, be prepared to cover the plants with burlap whenever rare frosts threaten.

OUTSIDE. If you do grow them outside in the ground, plant them shallowly in well-drained soil. Mulch plants with oak leaves or pine needles, and water only when the ground beneath the mulch dries out.

IN POTS. Vireyas like to be a bit root-bound. Leave them in the container you got them in until roots start coming out the drain hole. Then pot them up one size. They should be planted in a mix that's 1 part peat, 1 part ground bark, and 2 parts perlite or pumice.

EXPOSURE. Vireyas do best in places that get morning sun and filtered afternoon light. Keep them out of the wind. If you have only a poorly lit space indoors, supplement natural light with a grow light.

WATER. Drainage is critical, and overwatering kills Vireyas. One successful commercial grower recommends growing Vireyas in tall, slender pots to guarantee good drainage, then watering by weight: when potted Vireya feels light, water; when it's heavy (with water), leave it alone. To make water penetrate the potting mix better, treat the soil annually with a horticultural wetting agent.

FERTILIZER. Feed in spring, summer, and fall with an organic fertilizer such as cottonseed or alfalfa meal, or a custom blend from a Vireya specialist and occasionally add a quarter-strength dose of soluble 20-20-20 fertilizer when you water.

CHOICES TO GET YOU STARTED

If you've never grown Vireya rhododendrons, you may want to select from some that experienced growers have found easy to manage: 'Aravir', 'Calavar', 'Elizabeth Ann Seton', 'Hansa Bay', *R. jasminiflorum punctatum,* 'St. Valentine', 'Sweet Wendy', 'Triumphans', and 'Vladimir Bukovsky'.

Pests, Diseases, and Other Problems

Rare is the popular garden plant that will not be visited occasionally by one or more of the common garden pests and diseases. Many plant favorites may also play host now and then to pests or diseases that are specific to that particular plant. Azaleas, rhododendrons, and camellias are no exception—but note our use of the words "occasionally" and "now and then."

An enumeration of potential pests and diseases should be regarded as a source of information, not a suggestion of impending disaster. A number of problems are limited to certain regions; all occur only when conditions favor them. More often than not, poor health stems from poor culture or some sort of environmental problem. By learning to recognize the cultural conditions your plant needs and the symptoms of trouble, you should be able to ward off most problems before they become severe.

General problems

Many problems affect azaleas, rhododendrons, and camellias alike. Following are some of the most common problems, along with steps you can take to alleviate or eliminate them.

CATERPILLARS

These are most serious in the East, where they chew holes in leaves or chew off leaf margins. Damage is broader than the much smaller individual notches made by root weevils, and can be from *Lepidoptera* larvae or climbing cutworms and fruit worms. *Bacillus thuringiensis* (Bt) can take care of *Lepidoptera* larvae, and acephate or carbaryl can be used on the night-feeding cutworms and fruit worms.

CHLOROSIS

Plants with yellowish leaves are said to have chlorosis—often the result of a nutrient deficiency (usually iron, but sometimes magnesium or zinc). But it can also be caused by anything from insects to a bad transplanting job. A soil test can often tell you why your plants are chlorotic, or you can try to figure it out on your own.

Iron-deficiency chlorosis, the botanical equivalent of anemia, usually shows up on the new leaves of plants grown where the soil isn't acid enough. Iron may be present in the soil, but another substance, such as lime, may make it unavailable to the plant. (In the case of rhododendrons, the roots can absorb iron well enough, even from alkaline soil. But alkaline soil makes the plant have alkaline sap, which prevents iron from getting to the plant cells. The iron can't be assimilated and used by the cells until the soil, and thus the sap, is made more acid.)

If you suspect that your soil pH is too high, a good first step is to amend your soil with something like ferrous sulfate to pull the pH down into the ranges recommended for the plants you're growing (see the discussion of pH on page 81). Sometimes that alone frees up enough iron to make the plant function normally, and the chlorosis disappears in a few weeks.

If ferrous sulfate doesn't solve the problem, try spraying the leaves with chelated iron. If the leaves start to green up within a week, apply chelated iron to the soil for a longer-term fix.

When chlorosis is from magnesium deficiency, mature leaves often show reddish veins on their back sides. Try to correct it by spraying Epsom salts (magnesium sulfate) on the leaves at the rate of 2 tablespoons per 1 gallon of water. If leaves turn green, add magnesium sulfate crystals to the soil at the rate of 1 pound per 100 square feet.

For other kinds of nutrient-based chlorosis, an application of fritted trace elements may correct the problem. If none of these things works, the chlorosis may be caused by root rot or damage to roots from insect larvae, root loss from transplanting, or planting too deeply. Root loss will correct itself as new roots are generated, and deep planting can be corrected by raising the

Chlorosis on rhododendron

Sun bleaching on rhododendron

plant up. (If you don't raise the plant, and if it's not too deep, it will develop new surface roots and return to health.)

Don't confuse these problems with chlorosis caused by sun bleaching (that usually appears only on one side of the plant and can be corrected by giving the plant more shade), or with leaves that turn yellow before they drop off in spring. Healthy camellia and evergreen leaves usually live 2 to 3 years, though rhododendron leaves may live longer; camellia leaves die and drop in spring, rhododendron leaves from spring through fall.

DEER

Deer eat almost anything when they're hungry enough. They regularly munch on deciduous azaleas until they're above salad-bar height, and occasionally go after evergreen rhododendrons and Vireyas (especially *R. laetum*). Build an obstacle course of rhododendrons in front of the deciduous azaleas and you'll get protection from deer, as well as evergreen shrubs to conceal the woody stems of the deciduous plant in winter. Deer seem to avoid *C. japonica* varieties but go for other camellias.

Dozens of home and commercial remedies are used to deter deer, from hostile dogs to human hair to lion scat from the zoo, but only one is foolproof: a deer fence.

LEAF BURN

Leaf edges turn brown when plants have taken up too much salt—either from fertilizer, soil, or water. To leach any kind of excess salt from the soil, flush the root zone with water every few months by flooding it to saturation three times, letting it drain through each time.

If you're growing rhododendrons in a windy place, windburn can scorch leaf edges. The only solution for that is a windbreak (see page 103). Windburn is most common on young leaves, salt burn on older ones.

MITES

These tiny spiders that suck the juices out of plant leaves are so small that you'll probably see their damage or their webs on the undersides of the leaves before you see *them* (and that might take a magnifying glass). They're most common in hot, dry parts of the country.

Mite damage gives a stippled look to azalea and rhododendron leaves, and makes camellia foliage look dusty and gray. Overhead watering or hosing plants down helps wash dust off the foliage, and leaves the mites open to attack by predators.

Predatory mites can help with mite problems. These insects prey on damaging mites, not on plants; just remember that you can't use them in combination with insecticides. You can smother damaging mites with a spray of light horticultural oil when the temperature is expected to stay between 40°F/4°C and 85°F/29°C for a few days. Or spray them with insecticidal soap or a miticide such as dicofol in late spring.

TOP: Leaf scorch
BOTTOM: Rhododendron root rot

ROOT ROT

Warm weather and heavy, moist soil set up perfect conditions for various kinds of root rots. These occur across the United States, and together are among the most common causes of death for azaleas, rhododendrons, and camellias. Root rots are difficult to diagnose and virtually impossible to treat, but in many cases they can be easily prevented: just plant in soil that has good drainage and don't overwater. Irrigate plants with deep, infrequent watering instead of shallow, frequent watering. If a whole bed of shrubs looks chlorotic, suspect nutrient deficiency; if random mature plants look chlorotic or stressed, suspect root rot.

Oak root fungus (*Armillaria* species), which kills plants by cutting off the flow of nutrients and water between roots and trunk, is quite common in the Southeast and in low-elevation, nondesert parts of California. It usually strikes shrubs planted in an area where other plants (especially oaks) have died from the same disease. It can be passed from diseased roots—even ones that have been dead for a long time—to healthy roots.

Afflicted plants usually have dull green or yellowish leaves and thinning foliage. Leaves may wilt, and whole branches can die back as the disease advances. In late autumn, clumps of tan mushrooms may appear at the base of the trunk. If you look between the bark and the wood there, or even on larger roots just below ground level, you'll find a mat of white fungus.

You can remove soil from around the base of the trunk, exposing the union of root and trunk to the air, and cut out infected parts. But even so, the prognosis isn't good.

Phytophthora (there are many *Phytophthora* species) is the major root rot in the Pacific Northwest and an important problem in much of the rest of the country. It can kill most azaleas, rhododendrons, and camellias, but *C. sasanqua* and *C. oleifera* are resistant. The disease is carried by water and soil, and can be brought into gardens on nursery stock.

As the disease takes hold, it rots fibrous roots, then main roots, and finally the stem itself. Along the way, top growth stops, and leaves become chlorotic or dull and wilted; they hang onto the plant after they've died. When you dig up a plant killed by phytophthora, its roots will be brown with rot.

Affected plants can be treated with fosetyl-Al, which helps for as long as its use continues. If you want to raise camellias in infected soil, plant only *C. sasanqua* or *C. oleifera* varieties or other kinds of camellias grafted onto a *C. sasanqua* or *C. oleifera* understock. To grow rhododendrons in infected soil, amend the soil with 50 percent ground pine bark or peat before you plant.

ROOT WEEVILS

These weevils are about ¼ inch long and live in the soil around the roots of azaleas, rhododendrons, and camellias. The problem is most serious on rhododendrons in California, the Pacific Northwest, and in the northeastern quarter of the country. The weevils climb up into the leaves at night and notch their edges, then return to the ground and hide in the leaf litter under plants during the day. There are several similar kinds of weevils that feed on azaleas, rhododendrons, and camellias; some common ones are strawberry root weevils, black vine weevils, and obscure root weevils.

You can find adults at night by looking on and under plant leaves, or by shaking a rhododendron branch over a piece of white posterboard; the adults will fall off.

Many gardeners encircle the trunk with plastic food wrap, then coat it with a sticky insect barrier such as Tanglefoot; it keeps the weevils from climbing into the canopy at night. Others spray infested leaves with an insecticide such as cyfluthrin, bendiocarb, chlorpyrifos, or neem. The weevils will take it in as they eat and be poisoned. Neem is the most environmentally friendly of these pesticides, but it requires more frequent applications. Acephate also works but has a short residual life and may burn

TOP: Obscure root weevil and damage
BOTTOM: Scale

leaf tips. Spray at 3- to 4-week intervals from the time the first adults appear in late May or early June until damage stops.

The legless larvae show up in late summer and fall and feed on the roots. It is possible to control them by drenching plant roots with acephate, bendiocarb, or carbofuran, but you must apply the insecticide when the soil is warm and not wet, or it will wash out. Drenching is most effective on containerized plants and less so in the ground, where it's harder to get the chemical to completely infuse the infested soil. The larvae may also be controlled with beneficial nematodes, though they must be from vigorous stock (use a reputable supplier) and are becoming harder to find.

SOOTY MOLD

When you spot a black coating on azalea, rhododendron, or camellia leaves, chances are it's sooty mold, which grows on the sticky honeydew (excrement) of aphids, mealybugs, scale insects, and whiteflies. All these creatures are sucking insects. Most hide on the backs of leaves and give them a stippled or chlorotic look. To stop leaf damage and control the sooty mold, control the insects that are behind it all.

Aphids usually appear on tender new growth, often distorting it. You can repeatedly blast them off with a jet of water from a hose, or spray them with a mild pesticide such as insecticidal soap. It's a good idea to use the insecticidal soap anyway, because it does a good job washing sooty mold off the leaves.

Mealybugs are primarily a problem in the South. They're usually found in clusters, and unlike scale insects, they're mobile and may hide in fissures in the bark. Spray them with acephate, dimethoate, and oxydemeton-methyl; all have systemic properties that can reach unsprayed insects through the plant's sap.

Scale insects are so subtle you may miss them; they can look like bumpy irregularities on the bark, but some kinds (like the widespread cottony camellia scale, which affects both rhododendrons and camellias) leave cottony egg sacks on the leaves as evidence.

The immobile adult scales are protected by waxy shells. Sprays of light horticultural oil can smother the scales in spring and fall. Apply when temperatures are expected to remain between 40°F/4°C and 85°F/29°C for a few days. Scale insects are also vulnerable to systemic insecticides (ones that are taken up by the plant and sucked in by the scales), such as acephate, dimethoate, or oxydemeton-methyl. *You* can also act as a biological control, scraping scales off twigs and branches with a pocket knife. That helps, but it's long work.

Mobile young scales, called crawlers, are much easier to kill, if you can catch them when they're present, which isn't long. The timing varies from area to area but is usually during late spring and early summer. Call your county extension agent to find out when crawlers are active locally, then spray plants with insecticidal soap or a potent insecticide such as acephate, carbaryl, chlorpyrifos, or malathion.

Whiteflies are just that: tiny, white-winged flies whose immobile nymphs suck the juices from leaves and drop honeydew below. They're most common in the South and in California. Spray in summer with acephate, carbaryl, chlorpyrifos, or malathion at 2- to 3-week intervals.

Lace bug

TROUBLESHOOTING AZALEAS AND RHODODENDRONS

Like all plants, azaleas and rhododendrons are sometimes subject to problems specific to them. But only a few of the pests and diseases listed below are considered potentially serious, and of those, some appear only in specific regions of the country.

BUD BLIGHT

When azalea or rhododendron buds turn brown and are covered with black spores, bud blight *(Briosia azaleae)* is usually to blame. Just pick off infected buds and send them out with the trash or bury them.

Buds die for environmental reasons as well: very dry summers can kill buds, as can too much frost. In most cases the buds just die in place, not falling off until new growth appears the following spring.

LACE BUGS

In the East and especially in the South, where they produce multiple generations, lace bugs can decimate the foliage of evergreen azaleas, and to a lesser extent, deciduous azaleas and rhododendrons. In the Pacific Northwest, lace bug damage is possible, but rare. From the top, leaves look stippled or whitened; the undersides are dirty with frass (excrement) and shed skins. Eventually, the leaves turn yellow or brown and fall off. Eggs of lace bugs and some adults overwinter on the backs of the leaves, usually along the midribs, and larvae work along with the adults sucking the juices out of leaves.

Lace bugs are most serious on plants growing in full sun. Move plants to shade and the problem will diminish. You can control small infestations with repeated applications of horticultural oil (especially in winter) or insecticidal soap when adults and nymphs are present. (Aim for late March to early April in the South, when eggs hatch and overwintering adults are present;

later, farther north.) For heavier infestations, try acephate, carbaryl, chlorpyrifos, diazinon, dimethoate, or malathion.

Early treatment is best because it reduces later generations and prevents leaf injury that will look bad all year. Avoid treatment at flowering time, since it can ruin blooms. Be sure to spray the undersides of the leaves thoroughly.

LEAF AND FLOWER GALL

The leaf and flower gall fungus *(Exobasidium vaccinii)* makes a leaf thicken and develop a flowerlike structure that eventually hardens into a brown gall. Evergreen azaleas get it most often. The disease comes and goes, and can appear in any part of the country.

Cut the galls out when you see them and burn or bury them. If you have an azalea that's especially susceptible to gall, replace it with one that isn't.

LEAF MINERS

Most common on evergreen azaleas on the eastern seaboard and in the Ohio Valley, Northern California, and the Pacific Northwest, these creatures tunnel through leaves, then emerge and roll up the leaves, tying them with silk before they pupate and emerge as small moths. You can't do much with them at the miner stage, but after they emerge you can kill them with a spray of dimethoate.

LEAF SPOT

Leaf spot shows up on rhododendrons for any number of reasons, often from various fungus infections that follow leaf damage from sunburn, windburn, and drought. The spots commonly show up after a spell of wet weather and stop growing when dry weather comes.

If sunburn caused the damage that gave leaf spot a foothold, move your plant into a more shaded location. To treat existing leaf spot, spray with a fungicide.

Necrotic ring spot makes reddish brown rings or spots on the leaves and results from a virus. There is no treatment for it, but it doesn't seem to spread or cause serious trouble for the plant.

Some kinds of rhododendrons, including 'Mrs. G. W. Leak', have purplish leaf spots that are simply part of their makeup. These spots don't hurt the plants, and there's nothing you can do about them.

PETAL BLIGHT

Two kinds of petal blight can damage azalea and rhododendron flowers from time to time. Botrytis petal blight *(Botrytis cinerea)*, which is most common in the South, East, and Pacific Northwest, is a fungus that causes petals to develop water-soaked spots that later turn dry and papery. You can treat it by spraying the plant, covering buds and flowers, with captan or chloro-thalonil 2 or 3 times a week while flowers are opening.

Azalea petal blight *(Ovulinia azaleae),* which also affects rhododendrons, makes tiny water-soaked spots on petals that spread over the whole flower and work their way from the bottom of the plant to the top. Fully involved petals have a slimy feel. Small, black, pellet-like overwintering bodies (sclerotia) form on flowers a few weeks after infection, and eventually produce mushroomlike apothecia that start the cycle over again. Remove all infected flowers and bury them or send them out with the trash. You can also start a spray program with captan, chlorothalonil, PCNB, or triforine just before buds open.

POWDERY MILDEW

This appears on most deciduous azaleas late in the season, and a related mildew can show up on some rhododendrons anytime during the growing season. Humidity and shade promote the growth of powdery mildew, but water (especially daily overhead watering) inhibits it.

On deciduous azaleas, powdery mildew looks like fine white powder sprinkled on the leaves. Some varieties are more resistant than others.

On rhododendrons, powdery mildew makes pale yellow or brown patches on the leaves. A few kinds of rhododendrons, including 'Virginia Richards' and some of the Whitney hybrids, have serious trouble with it, but many more varieties aren't susceptible. Avoid vulnerable varieties if mildew is a problem in your garden.

STEM BORER

Stem borers are the larvae of clear-winged, wasplike moths that colonize rhododendrons in the East. They bore through the bark, usually of large rhododendrons, and through the area just inside the bark. When they badly damage or kill branches, the dead leaves hang on, as they do when root rot is the culprit. To gain control, you must spray after adults have emerged from the wood and before their young have hatched and bored back into the plant. Timing is everything: you have to put out a sex-attractant trap and spray about 10 days after you catch the first male moths (usually between May and July). The most effective spray is chlorpyrifos. If you don't want to follow this regimen, cut out and burn affected branches.

TOP: Azalea petal blight
BOTTOM: Mildew

THRIPS

Thrips appear in the South, in California, and on greenhouse plants everywhere. They feed on the undersides of leaves and cause mottling and chlorosis as they suck the juices out of the cells. You can spray them with acephate, chlorpyrifos, diazinon, or malathion. Spraying twice, 2 weeks apart, in late spring or early summer usually takes care of them.

TROUBLESHOOTING CAMELLIAS

Camellia growers are fortunate that so lovely a plant is so little bothered by pests or diseases. In fact, most camellia failures can be traced to poor cultural practices—which suggests that the camellia's number one problem is actually the gardener!

That's not to say that a camellia will never be visited by a few pests and diseases, but few will ever assault with such force as to warrant attempts at control. Following are the most common problems and the measures needed to control them, should you find it necessary.

BUD DROP

Some kinds of camellias set more flowers than they can support and naturally drop some of them before bloom. Other varieties drop buds when they're grown in borderline climates—ones where they normally have trouble flowering. In still other cases, bud drop is strictly an environmental problem that results from too much water, too little water, or sudden weather changes. Some varieties are more prone to drop buds than others, but most years it simply isn't a problem. If you get bud drop for more than 2 years in a row, consider changing varieties.

CANKER

Two cankers look and act alike, and have similar treatments.

Dieback *(Glomerella cingulata)* most commonly shows up in the South on all kinds of camellias; in the West, dieback from *Glomerella* is possible, but similar symptoms from *Phomopsis* (following page) are more common. Some camellias, such as 'Professor Charles S. Sargent', are resistant, while others, including 'Ville de Nantes', are especially susceptible.

Dieback often strikes before you know your plants have it, causing new growth (sometimes just a single shoot) to spontaneously die back. Leaves cling to the branch after they die. Within a few weeks, cankers open up at the base of dead shoots, on branches, or on the trunk, oozing pink spores during long stretches of wet weather. In spring, insects and splashing water may spread spores onto healthy camellias.

To control dieback, cut out all the cankered branches 6 inches below the lowest canker and spray camellias with a fungicide during the 2 months of spring leaf drop.

Phomopsis is more common in California, striking mostly *C. sasanqua* and some *C. reticulata* camellias. Treatment is the same as for *Glomerella* dieback; cut out cankered branches 6 to 12 inches below the lowest canker and spray camellias with a fungicide during the 2 months of spring leaf drop.

LEAF SCURF OR EDEMA

This disease most often affects camellias during cloudy, humid weather when the ground is wet and warmer than the air. Plants take up so much moisture that leaf cells form blisters and burst. As they heal, brown, elongated scabs form on the backs of the leaves.

Outside the Northwest, leaf scurf tends to appear on *C. reticulata* varieties and on plants that have large root systems and sparse foliage. Warmer, drier weather will solve the problem.

PETAL BLIGHT

This fungus, *Ciborinia camelliae*, is a worldwide phenomenon that affects all colors and species of camellias. Most common after very wet winters, it starts out as a small brown spot on a flower petal, then spreads until, a day later, the whole flower is brown and slimy to the touch. Normal, blight-free blossoms last 5 to 7 days; blighted blooms can be ruined in 1 or 2 days.

Petal blight does more damage to later-flowering camellias than to earlier ones, and does no harm to the plant itself. When only flower edges go brown, the problem is more likely damage from sun or drying winds.

The blight has no cure yet, but if you just practice good garden sanitation, you'll see markedly less petal blight over a 3- to 4-year period, especially if your neighbors are also fighting it (or

TOP: Thrips on rhododendron
BOTTOM: Flower blight

have no camellias). The blight spores can travel about 1½ miles; the farther you are from the source, the less trouble you should have with the fungus.

In gardens where the blight is well established, start by removing all the mulch under the camellias and sending it out with the trash or burying it under at least 5 inches of soil. Replace it with fresh mulch that includes no camellia flowers. From that point on, remove all faded flowers or pick them up off the ground and either send them out with the trash or bury them.

If you're desperate to save the blooms on a single plant, you can spray the plant with a fungicide such as chlorothalonil. It's also possible to stop growth of the apothecia (mushrooms) that release the blight-causing spores by drenching the soil with a fungicide such as captan or PCNB.

VIRUSES

Camellia viruses are everywhere and almost never kill the plant. Some are cultivated to variegate camellia leaves and flowers. (Virus-induced variegation usually produces flowers with spots, blotches, or cross-petal stripes—though they occasionally run lengthwise; and leaves with yellow or cream flecks or blotches. Genetic variegation usually produces flowers with lengthwise striping and white leaf variegation.)

The most visible symptom of a virus is usually yellowish leaves, but that can also indicate anything from iron deficiency to sun scorch. Sometimes, however, you can diagnose a virus by eliminating every other possibility. If your camellia is planted in red earth, it is almost certainly getting enough iron. If you feed with trace elements occasionally and if your soil's pH is in the 5.5 to 6.5 range, the plant is probably getting enough trace elements. If it's shaded during the heat of the day, you can eliminate sun scorch. And if your soil drains well enough to rule out root rot, and if there are no other obvious diseases, a virus may be the problem.

The best treatment is consistently good care (feeding, mulching, watering, pest control, and pruning) to minimize the virus's effect on the plant's overall health. The next best treatment is to replace the affected plant with one you like better.

INDEX

Numerals in **boldface** refer to color photographs. For individual hybrid names, see the showcases.